SIMPLIFIED STRATEGY SKILLS

Foundations of strategic thinking through
THE BHAGAVAD GITA

Dr. Atul Kumar Bansal

BlueRoseONE.com
Stories Matter
NewDelhi • London

BLUEROSE PUBLISHERS
India | U.K.

BlueRose ONE.com
Stories Matter
NewDelhi • London

For permissions requests or inquiries regarding this publication, please contact:

BLUEROSE PUBLISHERS
www.BlueRoseONE.com
info@bluerosepublishers.com
+91 8882 898 898
+4407342408967

ISBN: 978-93-7018-963-8

Cover design: Yash Singhal
Typesetting: Namrata Saini

First Edition: August 2025

Table of Contents

About the Book

'Simplified Strategy Skills - Foundations of Strategic Thinking Through the Bhagavad Gita' offers a unique approach to strategic leadership by bridging ancient wisdom with modern business challenges. In this insightful work, author Atul Kumar Bansal draws from the timeless teachings of the Bhagavad Gita to illuminate fundamental principles of effective strategy that transcend time and context.

The book explores fifteen essential dimensions of strategic thinking, ranging from clarity of purpose and detachment from results to resilience, ethical conduct, and risk management. Each chapter provides specific wisdom extracted from the Bhagavad Gita and demonstrates its practical application to contemporary business scenarios, providing leaders with both philosophical depth and actionable guidance.

Unlike conventional strategy books that focus primarily on external analysis and competitive positioning, Bansal's approach emphasizes that strategic mastery begins with self-mastery. The leader, able to cultivate internal clarity, ethical steadfastness, and emotional resilience will naturally make better strategic decisions when facing external challenges.

Particularly valuable in today's volatile, uncertain, complex, and ambiguous business environment, the book offers a framework that helps leaders navigate complexity with wisdom and purpose. Whether you're a C-suite executive steering organizational transformation, a middle manager implementing strategic initiatives, or an emerging leader developing your capabilities, *Simplified Strategy Skills* provides a compass for your strategic journey. One that integrates ancient philosophical insights with practical business applications.

Building on the success of his previous work, *'Simplified Management Skills - Lessons from the Ramayana'*, Bansal continues his exploration of how India's philosophical heritage can enhance modern business practice, offering readers a distinctive perspective that combines timeless wisdom with contemporary relevance.

About the Author

Atul Kumar Bansal has over 30 years of experience in developing Information Technology, large-scale transformation projects, digital strategy, and security blueprints for organizations with short-term and long-term strategies in alignment with business objectives.

A Strategic Digital Technology executive, Atul is passionate and well-versed in transforming organizations using information technology. He has been recognized with multiple industry accolades including the CIO-100 Award (IDG), Innovative CIO, Iconic CIO Award (IDC), Digital Warrior by DataQuest, and Eminent CIO of India, among others. Throughout his distinguished career, he has served as CIO with multiple leading organizations.

With more than 30 years of professional, technical, commercial, and functional leadership experience, Atul has developed expertise across numerous domains including IT Strategy, IT Policy, Large-scale Transformation Projects, Program Governance, Digital Strategy, RPA, IoT, Digitization & Digitalization, ERP Implementation, Operations Management, and Change Management. He has initiated multiple projects that enable businesses to enhance their operations while providing improved user IT experiences and increasing revenue. Atul has spearheaded large-scale transformation programs across multiple sectors, effectively engaging various stakeholders at all levels to drive IT and related business process integration while leading necessary change management efforts across organizations.

Atul specializes in defining IT Policy, IT Cyber Security Policy, and Digitization Strategy. He firmly believes that digitization and digitalization are key to enhancing business prospects and increasing customer satisfaction.

Currently, Atul serves as Group Head IT for Gateway Distriparks Limited. His previous book, ***'Simplified Management Skills - Lessons from the Ramayana'*** explored how ancient wisdom from the Ramayana can be applied to modern management practices. With ***'Simplified Strategy Skills - Foundations of Strategic Thinking Through the Bhagavad Gita',*** Atul continues his journey of connecting timeless Indian philosophical teachings with contemporary business challenges, offering readers a unique perspective that bridges ancient wisdom and modern strategic thinking.

Acknowledgments

Writing this book turned into a journey far more fulfilling than I ever imagined. I've come to understand that our world truly comes alive when people commit to growth and leadership, and it burns even brighter when they sacrifice their time to mentor others. My sincere appreciation goes to everyone willing to advance with determination toward personal development while lifting others along the way.

I owe special thanks to my extraordinary wife, Preeti Bansal, who stood by me unfailingly, reviewed rough drafts, and offered crucial advice on cover designs with patience and grace, even while our little one constantly pulled me away from work with adorable distractions.

My greatest debt of gratitude belongs to our respected CMD of Gateway Distriparks Limited, Shri Prem Kishan Gupta, alongside my colleagues, whose unwavering support and motivation through their real-world experiences made all the difference. Their guidance transformed this manuscript from mere aspiration into reality.

So many generous souls contributed their valuable time and insights, playing crucial roles in breathing life into these pages. I extend my heartfelt appreciation to each one. Their contributions elevated this book beyond what I could have achieved alone.

To my dedicated beta readers, I offer sincere gratitude. Your careful analysis and thoughtful suggestions undoubtedly enriched every chapter of this work.

I want to express profound thanks to my daughters Aditi Bansal and Anushka Bansal, and my son, Ayush Bansal, for their brilliant recommendations and countless hours of diligent proofreading that significantly elevated the quality of this book.

Finally, I would like to thank all readers of this book. It is because of you that I have had the opportunity to create this book, ***Simplified Strategy Skills***.

Thank you all, from the depths of my heart. I feel truly grateful and blessed!

Dedication

To the memory of my late beloved ***Mother and Father****.*

Your love & blessings remain the cornerstone of everything I strive to achieve.

Introduction

In today's complex and rapidly changing business environment, leaders at all levels face unprecedented challenges. The velocity of technological advancement, shifting global markets, evolving customer expectations, and increasing stakeholder demands create a landscape where traditional approaches to strategy often fall short. Amid this complexity, we find ourselves searching for wisdom that transcends time; principles that remain relevant regardless of era or context.

The Bhagavad Gita, one of humanity's oldest philosophical texts, offers such timeless wisdom. Though composed thousands of years ago on an ancient battlefield, its teachings speak directly to the modern executive confronting today's business battlegrounds. This convergence of ancient wisdom and contemporary challenges forms the foundation of 'Simplified Strategy Skills'.

This book emerged from the recognition that beneath the complexity of modern strategic frameworks lies a set of fundamental principles that great leaders have always understood. The dialogue between Lord Krishna and Arjuna on the battlefield of Kurukshetra offers great insights into these principles which includes clarity of purpose, detachment from results, adaptability, ethical leadership, resilience, and strategic execution among others.

As you journey through this book, you'll discover how the Gita's teachings can transform your approach to a business strategy. The first chapters establish core philosophical foundations; like the importance of purpose clarity, action without attachment to outcomes, and the adaptability that comes from true knowledge. These concepts aren't mere philosophical abstractions but practical tools that today's leaders can apply to enhance their strategic thinking.

The middle sections translate these philosophical foundations into leadership applications: how to delegate effectively, build resilience, maintain ethical standards, and focus your attention amid distractions. These chapters bridge ancient wisdom with contemporary leadership challenges, showcasing how ancient principles are timeless.

The final chapters explore specialized domains of strategic management which includes planning and execution, conflict resolution, human resource management, team building, stakeholder engagement, change management, leadership development, and risk management. In each domain, we find that the Gita's wisdom provides unexpected clarity and practical guidance.

This book is intended for leaders who sense that conventional strategic frameworks, while useful, may be insufficient for navigating today's complex challenges. It's for those who recognize that effective strategy requires not just analytical tools but also inner development, clarity of mind, steadiness of purpose, ethical foundations, and emotional resilience.

Whether you're a CEO guiding organizational transformation, a middle manager implementing strategic initiatives, or an emerging leader developing your strategic capabilities, this book offers both philosophical depth and practical application. The approach is deliberately simplified. Not because strategy is simple, but because beneath the complexity lie fundamental principles that, once understood, illuminate the path forward.

As we explore these fifteen dimensions of strategic thinking, we'll discover that the Bhagavad Gita doesn't just offer philosophical comfort. It provides practical wisdom for navigating our most challenging strategic dilemmas. By connecting this ancient wisdom with contemporary challenges, we'll uncover a framework for strategic thinking that integrates external action with internal development, analytical precision with ethical awareness, and immediate concerns with long-term vision.

Let us begin this journey of discovery, where the battlefield wisdom of ancient India illuminates the boardroom challenges of today's global economy.

CHAPTER 1

Clarity of Purpose (Sankhya Yoga)

Imagine yourself on a battlefield of life where you are faced with a daunting set of problems that makes you question and deliberate upon what your next move should be. This was the struggle of Arjuna, famous warrior from the Mahabharata. Doubt, fear and deep uncertainty had made Arjuna's chariot come to a standstill in the heat of a massive conflict. Should he do his duty as a warrior or should he take a step back from the mayhem? It is in this pivotal moment that Lord Krishna becomes his mentor, offering guiding principles that have aided people to this very day.

The Bhagavad Gita consists of these deep conversations between Krishna and Arjuna and within these explorations, purpose is found deeply. What Krishna emphasizes in his teachings is the need to be aware of one's place in life and act upon it.

These teachings are no different in the modern world than they were on the battlefield of Kurukshetra. It is immaterial whether you are an individual needing guidance or a leader of a certain organization, knowing your purpose is the foundation of your strategy and action.

Be it anything, the central question is the purpose of taking the action i.e. knowing the why. Why do you do? What you do? What drives you? In the case of Arjuna, this lay in understanding his Dharma - his responsibility as a soldier serving on the side of justice. Similarly, for us, it could mean directing our self-objectives to something bigger than us within our jobs, love and society.

A powerful shloka from the Gita reminds us:

"Karmanye vadhikaraste ma phaleshu kadachana ma karma phala hetur bhurma te sango stva karmani"

कर्मण्येवाधिकारस्ते मा फलेषु कदाचन।
मा कर्मफलहेतुर्भूर्मा ते सङ्गोऽस्त्वकर्मणि॥

Do your duty, but never attach yourself to the fruits of your work. Never work for rewards, but keep fulfilling your duty.

In this chapter, we will begin by evaluating concepts from Gita and blend it with practical techniques, which in turn will make the ancient knowledge easier to understand and relevant. Moreover, we will discuss accounts of Mahabharata, which will demonstrate the process through which Arjuna evolved from being confused to the state of enlightenment. This can now help tackle numerous challenges during one's lifetime.

You will feel that you have a clear purpose by the end of this chapter; whether you are a leader, an entrepreneur, or even an ordinary person wanting to bring meaning to their everyday life, the principles discussed are going to be very helpful. This chapter will be inspirational, as it aligns with the teachings from the Gita in a manner that will help understand their purpose clearly, stating the fact that it's not only about strategy but if anything, is the very core to strategizing.

Defining Purpose and Setting Goals

Understanding Purpose

Between two huge armies and amidst the great battlefield of Kurukshetra, Arjuna stood on his chariot. Seeing the faces of his family, friends and gurus on both sides, grief clouds him and he is plagued with doubt. How can he fight with those who he loves? The dilemma weighed him down leaving him half paralyzed: waffling on what he should do and for what the battle was being fought. At this moment of hopelessness, lord Krishna, his best friend gave to Arjuna the wisdom to reflect deeply about what his role and responsibilities are. Arjuna had been hesitant, and according to Krishna: he did not know his purpose. His Dharma as a warrior urged him to take action against injustice and uphold righteousness despite personal attachment. Krishna's wisdom enabled Arjuna to step away from his immediate feelings and understand what needed to be done for the greater good.

In this moment of confusion, Krishna shared a timeless shloka:

"Vyavasayatmika buddhir ekeha kurunandana bahushakha hy anantash ca buddhayo vyavasayinam"

व्यवसायात्मिका बुद्धिरेकेह कुरुनन्दन।
बहुशाखा ह्यनन्ताश्च बुद्धयोऽव्यवसायिनाम्॥

Those who are on this path are resolute in purpose, and their aim is one. O beloved child of the Kurus, the intelligence of those who are irresolute is many branched.

This story essentially iterates the need of purpose to overcome challenges, and make the right decisions. Clarity on 'why we do things', personal or professional, brings focus and inner strength in our life. Just like how Arjuna has to understand his place, take it upon himself & do it, when our actions are purpose driven, we are courageous enough to march forward even if there is uncertainty about where this will take us.

Fundamental Questions

Arjuna was asked profound questions by Krishna which are still applicable in this day and age:

What is your duty in this present moment?

How it contributes to the greater good, when you have fulfilled it?

Have you considered what values should govern your actions?

These type of questions are like a compass that help everyone who is looking for direction in life. They tell us to step back and think about what is on our plate. These questions are timeless in relevancy, whether you are leading an organization, leading a team or making your life decisions - these questions are extremely powerful in today's world.

Another teaching from the Gita says:

"Sreyan sva-dharmo vigunah para-dharmat sv-anusthitat sva-dharme nidhanam sreyah para-dharmo bhayavahah"

श्रेयान् स्वधर्मो विगुणः परधर्मात्स्वनुष्ठितात्।
स्वधर्मे निधनं श्रेयः परधर्मो भयावहः॥

Better to do your own duty imperfectly than to do another's duty perfectly. Better to die doing your own duty than to live doing another's.

If we are to get clarity on our duty, then we ask:

What can I bring that is singular & specific to this instance?

For Arjuna, as a warrior for us, it may be having the role of a mentor/ decision maker/problem solver. To acknowledge that the fulfilment of my duty is for the good of all directs us from a mindset of self-serving to community benefit.

It allows for meaningful action with a purpose and tied to a grand vision.

Finally, when actions are supported by strong values, then the ways make the ends honourable. This helps us make wise decisions about honesty, integrity and compassion.

The everlasting questions and answers are our counsellors that help us navigate through the complexities of life and help us to have clarity on uncertain situations.

Setting Goals

After understanding your purpose, there will be a few actionable and quantifiable goals to work with. Krishna exhorted Arjuna to perform his part not only in performing but also to say the steps involved in exact performance. There are 3 major elements that goal setting includes:

- Breaking the vision: Arjuna is fighting to uphold Dharma (as his ultimate goal) but he has to win the war to do so. Likewise, we must deconstruct our grand purpose into a series of down-sized goals to keep us on track to the bigger vision.
- Prioritization of actions: Long-term goals are great, but you need to figure out the first steps that will help progress toward that end. For Arjun, this meant concentrating on each part of the battle individually as

a step towards the common goal and tackling each difficulty one by one. In contemporary terms, prioritization enables us to prioritize tasks that drive us towards our goals.

- Making goals measurable: Same as for Arjuna who had to assess battlefield conditions to know where he stands, today's leaders and the destined to lead also can use metrics to measure progress. Ambitious, measurable goals offer a pathway and clarity of progress for us.

Through these things, we convert our vision into doable steps. Goals are way-stations that help one persevere. Goals make us feel empowered and we are able to take focused, consistent actions that drive actual outcomes aligned with a defined purpose.

As Krishna teaches in the Gita:

"Saknotihaiva yah sodhum prak sarira-vimoksanat kama-krodhodbhavam vegam sa yuktah sa sukhi narah"

शक्नोतीहैव यः सोढुं प्राक्शरीरविमोक्षणात्।
कामक्रोधोद्भवं वेगं स युक्तः स सुखी नरः॥

One who can control the urges of desire and anger before leaving the body is a yogi and is happy.

Avoiding Distractions

Distraction can lay even the best of plans in jeopardy. For Arjuna, his first distraction was his overwhelming desire for relationships and hatred of conflict. The burden of fighting with his own kin, and the resulting emotional clouding made him wonder his place. But Krishna instructed Arjuna to get over these distractions, as his purpose was bigger: his purpose as a warrior was to fight for justice, for dharma. In this contextual time where distraction stems from social media or due to competing priorities and self-doubt. In order to eliminate distractions, we must stay true to our grand vision. The lesson that Krishna teaches to Arjuna is to hold emotion in check and act in accordance to purpose. This includes:

- Refresh your mission: Reminding yourself of why you are doing this in the first place helps to keep commitment and focus.
- Establish boundaries: When to turn off time on unimportant tasks, or activities so you can focus on what is important.
- Mindfulness: Stay in the present moment and external noise is not taken as real which helps in clarity.

Krishna explains this wisdom in a beautiful shloka:

"Indriyani parany ahur indriyebhyah param manah manasas tu para buddhir yo buddheh paratas tu sah"

इन्द्रियाणि पराण्याहुरिन्द्रियेभ्यः परं मनः।
मनसस्तु परा बुद्धिर्यो बुद्धेः परतस्तु सः॥

The senses are higher than the body, the mind higher than the senses, the intelligence higher than the mind, and the soul is higher than the intelligence.

Arjuna going from a question to confidence in his mission shows that the only way to battle distractions is with strong vision, willpower and persistence on your goal. Focusing on our purpose and cutting out the superfluous distractions, will help tackle difficulties in a more effective and purposeful manner.

Practical Example

A modern-day leader should find their way, reading through the chapter of Arjuna's spiritual enlightenment. Think about a CEO through the wriggle of difficult organizational transformation. The CEO, just like Arjuna may have his share of the naysayers, the market uncertainty and emotional battering of attempting to execute change. Still, the CEO needs to remain goal oriented and in service of larger purpose. Start with clarity like Arjuna who laid out his vision to elaborate his duty towards dharma. For the CEO, it could be calling out the change needed, whether that means switching to new technologies or expanding into new business domains. Then break this vision into individual steps so each function knows what is required for the transformation.

Shifting the team on common goals is a critical component of this. Just as Arjuna rallied his inner battle toughness to be purposeful in combat, CEO needs to motivate the employees that will benefit that change. The CEO should track progress periodically. Metrics and KPIs to provide measurable insights that help in the alignment of short-term actions with long-term objectives. This is how Arjuna transformed to act, as he assessed the battle-ground with in his fray with Krishna. Through the teachings of the Gita, leaders can find their own Kurukshetra: navigate resistance and distraction and steer organizations clear of oblivion for sustainable success. Here Arjuna's tale is to be taken always along as an eternal manual of focus and clarity with regard to acting on today's problems.

Duty (Dharma) as Strategic Direction

Concept of Dharma

Dharma, as Krishna had told Arjuna, is knowing his own nature; the core of intent from which one focuses on direction and purpose. It is the duties and moral responsibilities associated with one position in life which form a governing morality, it urges your spirit to choose between right and wrong for decision making and crisis response. Arjuna (to himself): My Dharma (duty) as a warrior is to maintain the balance between justice and righteousness even if it comes at the cost of self-sacrifice. Krishna said the balance of life requires knowing and acting according to one's Dharma but, as to Arjuna, he must not shirk duty and the role it plays in maintaining balance even by fear or sorrow. Arjuna's concern on the other hand was because of his affection and commitment invested in his human likes. The knowledge of Krishna helped him see through the storm and rage to his place in keeping water from overflowing.

Krishna emphasizes this truth in a powerful shloka:

"Tasmad asaktah satatam karyam karma samacara asakto hy acaran karma param apnoti purusah"

तस्मादसक्तः सततं कार्यं कर्म समाचर।

असक्तो ह्याचरन्कर्म परमाप्नोति पुरुषः॥

Therefore, without being attached to the fruits of activities, one should act as a matter of duty, for by working without attachment, one attains the Supreme.

Dharma to the modern man could be fulfilling your duties of work and of personal life with honesty & responsibility. For example, a leader's Dharma may be knowing that you have to do the hard things for your team. A parent might live a Dharma of parenting, the teacher has his Dharma to teach, a person might live a Dharma of being child-friendly. Dharma helps us to connect our actions with something larger, something fulfilling and purposeful. While it inspires us to act on a higher, simpler impulse, rather than looking only for our own gratification. Living in Dharma means, we contribute for the well-being of our environment and it also sets the stage for success that is sustainable.

Strategic Responsibilities

In today's world, Dharma means strategic responsibilities. Take Bhishma in the Mahabharata, who stuck to his vow of protecting the Kuru dynasty, no matter what. His unwavering commitment to his duty is an example of strategic clarity even during personal challenges.

Bhishma's sense of responsibility shows us the importance of being true to our role and obligations even in adversity. For leaders, this means being accountable for our decisions, actions and making sure they align with the bigger picture. Bhishma's story teaches us that strategic clarity means more than just knowing what to do, it means having the will to do it with integrity and determination.

A shloka that captures this essence:

"Yadrsam kurute rupam tadrsam pratipasyati prakrtim svam avastabhya karoty esa vyavastthitih"

यदृशं कुरुते रूपं तदृशं प्रतिपश्यति।
प्रकृतिं स्वामवष्टभ्य करोत्येष व्यवस्थितिः॥

Whatever form one meditates upon, that one becomes. This is the eternal way of things.

Modern leaders can do the same. A CEO going through a major transformation will face resistance from employees, market uncertainty or personal doubts. But staying focused on the objective, being transparent and making decisions based on long term benefits will help navigate through those challenges.

When individuals and leaders understand and accept their strategic responsibilities, they are able to make decisions that are in the best interest of the overall good. Just as Bhishma did, we also must uphold our dharma and ensure that our actions are characterized by purpose, values and resilience in the face of difficulties.

Leadership Examples

Leadership is about juggling multiple responsibilities and making decisions that affect others. Krishna's teachings are great for leaders in complex situations. Here's how dharma as strategic responsibility shows up in modern leadership:

A manager's dharma: Supporting your team in crisis means keeping morale and productivity in balance. For example, in an economic downturn, a manager might focus on transparent communication, offer emotional support to employees while figuring out how to keep the business running.

A business leader's dharma: Making profit with ethics and community. For example, a CEO leading a company towards sustainability might prioritize green initiatives even if it means short term financial losses. By focusing on long term benefits like brand and customer loyalty, the leader aligns profit with purpose.

The Gita offers guidance for such leadership decisions:

"Yad yad acarati sresthas tat tad evetaro janah sa yat pramanam kurute lokas tad anuvartate"

यद्यदाचरति श्रेष्ठस्तत्तदेवेतरो जनः।

स यत्प्रमाणं कुरुते लोकस्तदनुवर्तते॥

Whatever action is performed by a great man, common men follow in his footsteps. And whatever standards he sets by exemplary acts, all the world pursues.

These examples show how leaders can move with clear strategy keeping their dharma, their guiding duty, at the forefront. This way of leading builds trust and strength, and makes a good impact that fits with what the organization and society want. When leaders follow their dharma, they push others to act with purpose and do the right thing. This helps everyone succeed while sticking to their values and vision.

Benefits

When leaders act on their purpose, it has a positive impact beyond an immediate response. A leader who knows his or her purpose, inspires the trust and collaboration of the team. Trust is crucial for effective leadership, which allows for open communication and shared commitment to common goals. Following one's own purpose also increases resilience. Leaders who know what they are supposed to do, and therefore what their purpose is, are better equipped to deal with challenges and to guide their teams through the unknown. This inner strength enables them to keep going and motivates others at low points. Decision making that is driven by purpose and values is likely to lead to long term growth and stability. Ethical practices, fairness and a commitment to the higher purpose guarantee that success is sustainable. Dharma as a strategy enables leaders to walk the talk. This tells them to act with integrity, identify what really matters, and leadership becomes a force for the best: *A force that benefits people and organizations.*

Strategic Alignment with Organizational Vision

Importance of Alignment

Krishna taught Arjuna an important lesson that is relevant to the fight's context as well as the present era. He taught him how one should always look towards the figure that is bigger than oneself. Selfish decisions should not be made, rather all choices must focus on justice and righteousness being served to a higher extent. This idea is especially crucial these days when organizations are working towards their objectives.

A beautiful shloka from the Gita emphasizes this:

"Atmany eva ca santustah tasya karyam na vidyate na casya sarva-bhutesu kascid artha-vyapasrayah"

आत्मन्येव च संतुष्टः तस्य कार्यं न विद्यते।
न चास्य सर्वभूतेषु कश्चिदर्थव्यापस्रयः॥

For one who is satisfied with the self, whose mind is steady and senses controlled, for whom the self is the only goal, there is no work to be done.

The starting point to a solution is clarity. The company should resolve on its exact long-term vision which will serve as a foundation during any strategic decision making. Communicating this vision to all staff members is a crucial step that the employees on every level of the organization are on board and in unison with the leaders. The mindset of each individual becomes broader and it makes more sense to strive toward a larger goal, hence they also feel more engaged in their work.

It's not just about understanding, but also taking action and applying it to the right projects to make real change happen. Krishna made it clear to Arjuna that he should think beyond the scope of his task. It's the same principle. Priorities must be straightened out, new goals set, and then under well-defined goals, the necessary steps for their achievement planned.

Alignment also raises morale. When people are stretched and inspired, they become more engaged, motivated. It makes the work more significant, and people are more positive and productive at work. This also helps in promoting teamwork because when all the people have a single aim, then the departments become less significant and people work efficiently in groups. It is easy for the teams to work together, share their talents and address a challenge or come up with a new idea. Last of all, strategic alignment needs to be continuously assessed and adapted. Just as Krishna reminded Arjuna of his duty, leaders have to constantly remind their teams what it is they are doing for the organization's overall purpose. Thus, organizations build up a community of people who are goal-orientated and would be successful even in the most unpredictable world.

Steps for Alignment

The goal of the Pandavas in the Mahabharata was to restore justice and establish a just and ethical rule. To achieve this, they had to work together seamlessly with every single person contributing towards the goal. We learn important lessons from their story to help us work well in teams or organizations today.

Each of the Pandava brothers had a job that was most suitable for him:

- The oldest brother, Yudhishthira led the group, and practiced diplomacy and doing what was right.
- Bhima, having incredible strength and determination was the source of courage and persistence on the battlefield and of the team's determination to keep going.
- Arjuna with Krishna, planned carefully and was meticulous about the challenges of the battle, not losing sight of the goal.

From their example, three steps to align a team are apparent:

Just as each of the Pandava's had a role, leaders should make it a point to ensure that each of the team members know what is expected of them. Confusion should be avoided and people should be accountable for their work through clear roles.

Working Together: Alignment means that all the work done should be directed towards the same objective. It also helps in breaking down the barriers between the different teams and promotes collaboration.

Ongoing Support: Just as Krishna spurred Arjuna to keep his eye on the big picture, leaders should often remind their team members how the work they are doing on a daily basis relates to the big picture of the mission. This is to ensure that everyone is on the right track.

Krishna teaches the value of this teamwork in the Gita:

"Sahayajnah prajah srstva purovaca prajapatih anena prasavisyadhvam esa vo 'stv ista-kamadhuk"

सहयज्ञः प्रजाः सृष्ट्वा पुरोवाच प्रजापतिः।
अनेंन प्रसविष्यध्वं एष वोऽस्त्विष्टकामधुक्॥

In the beginning of creation, the Lord created mankind, along with sacrifices for Vishnu, and said: By means of sacrifice will you prosper and gain all your desires.

The above steps aid the entire organization to work towards a common goal with least amount of conflict and in the most efficient manner in the long run.

Impact

This tells us that the Pandavas did not just form a team for no reason; a team is formed by goal orientation and effective planning. So, for this purpose, following are some of the lessons which can be derived for the modern organizations:

Having the Right Leadership: Just as the Pandavas came together for justice, organizations should have the right leadership to motivate and direct the people. A strong vision acts as a frame of reference and ensures that all efforts are directed towards the attainment of a common goal.

Define Job Descriptions: Each one of the Pandava brothers had a job that he was supposed to do based on what he could do best; Yudhishthira was the wise one, Bhima was the strong one and Arjuna was the strategic one. In order to get the most from a team it is very important to ensure that every member knows what is expected of him or her and how best to apply his or her skills.

Promote Teamwork: The Pandavas were successful because they worked together and used their strengths to overcome problems. Organizations can only succeed if they make teamwork their core value just as individualism is not encouraged.

A final shloka from the Gita reminds us:

"Saha-jam karma kaunteya sa-dosam api na tyajet sarvarambha hi dosena dhumenagnir ivavrtah"

सहजं कर्म कौन्तेय स-दोषम् अपि न त्यजेत्।

सर्वारम्भा हि दोषेण धूमेनाग्निरिवावृत:॥

One should not abandon duties born of one's nature, even if one sees defects in them, O son of Kunti. All endeavours are covered by some fault, just as fire is covered by smoke.

When people are going in the same direction, organizations become strong and stable. It is through collaboration that every effort, no matter how small, is directed towards the achievement of a common goal. It improves productivity, increases team work, and creates an organizational culture that is vital for lasting performance.

Conclusion

This is evident in Arjuna's trip and Krishna's lessons. This therefore provides a basis for a problem solver when having or dealing with problems, especially in times of confusion. This well-defined goal also helps in motivating other people. Clarity is constantly obtained through a process of self-reflection and personal growth, says the Bhagavad Gita. We should strive to improve our understanding of our goal no matter how much, just as Arjuna did, from being uncertain to being determined. The topic of the next chapter will be not to be to result oriented, and how one should focus on the process, not the result, in order to build up one's character.

CHAPTER 2

Detachment From Results (Karma Yoga)

This chapter will dive into another one of the teachings of the *Gita*, i.e. *Karma Yoga* or the "*Path of Selfless Service*". Here Lord Krishna emphasizes the importance of karma in life. He reveals that it is important for every human being to engage in some sort of activity in this material world. Further, he creates a distinction between the kinds of actions that lead to bondage and the kinds that lead to liberation. Those persons who continue to perform their respective duties externally for the pleasure of the Supreme without any attachment to its rewards achieve liberation at the end.

Karma Yoga is a practice of disciplining the senses where you direct all your senses to the action *(Karma)* and detach yourself from the fruits or result of that action.

A famous *shloka* of *Gita* says:

"Karmany-eva dhikaraste ma phaleshu kadachana ma karma-phala-hetur bhurma te sango'stvakarmani"

कर्मण्येवाधिकारस्ते मा फलेषु कदाचन।
मा कर्मफलहेतुर्भूर्मा ते सङ्गोऽस्त्वकर्मणि।।

You're only entitled to 'do the karma*' not to the fruit of* Karma. *Nor should you be attached to the* Karma *because the fruit of* karma *is not in your control. So, better dedicate your entire might to* Karma *and relinquish the thought of fruit.*

While actions form the very substance of our life without which life would cease to bear its nature- bitter or sweet. We cannot live one second without doing Karma, as even when we're thinking or sleeping, we are doing an action.

Remember only those actions that enhance your inner beauty, that purify your soul, that cleans your internal CPU and energizes you to give out to the world, because these are the actions that befit your Karma.

Definitely, it's easier said than done. How to detach from the fruit of Karma when Karma is itself done to get a specific result?

In fact, all the certifications, jobs, videos today are meant to upskill yourself. Although gaining knowledge and wisdom is itself a part of *Jnana Yoga.* But Money has always been the end of the means. It is crucial for survival. Indeed, if we forget to perform the duty at work, and go on helping others, we are neglecting our very first need of survival, nourishing our body.

But *Lord Krishna* didn't budge from giving us a way out of the *karma* web. He gave us the art of detachment.

The term "*self-less service*" doesn't necessarily imply free work for others. It is doing the work intended for you without any longing for the fruits of this work for the "*self.*" This is extremely difficult not only because it is our conditioning to be attached to the benefits for *me, I and myself,* but determining what activities are proper or improper requires being deeply in tune with one's intuition or self.

In fact, it could be argued that our contemporary life encourages the exact opposite of Krishna. From an early age, many of us are taught to do things to *get* a star in our notebooks, to be good to *get* presents, to get a higher education to *get* a good job, to get a good job to make lots of money, to make lots of money so you can buy lots of things to live more comfortably and do what you want to do, to dress in fashion to be liked or admired by others, to be famous or important to be "*someone*", basically everything to try to satisfy the little self superficially with material success rather than the big self.

However, the fact is that when we do good things we feel good inside. If we hurt or lie there is a tiny place inside us that gets hurt or is lied to. We must do our duties in life because they are our duties. In addition, we must do our best when performing our duties because it feels good to do our best.

Dear reader, it is important to understand that *Karma Yoga* stands for detachment from results, and not detachment from *Karma* itself.

We have full control over the results, as an enlightened being. But, we also have the *prarabdh* i.e. the fate, which is nothing more than the results of the karma (good or bad) in our past years, or even the past lives.

So, the *prarabdh* of achieving, or not achieving something today depends not only on the karma of the present, but also the karma of the past. What is in our hand is that we can only go on with doing the karma (*of course, good karma yields good results and vice versa*). And that karma we do must be with full force and dedication, yet devoid of the attachment with the results.

Detachment from the results will negate all ill effects (*despair, jealousy, depression etc.*) from our psyche, and we can lead a happier life.

Detachment doesn't imply that you don't *care* about results, you just don't *worry* about it. You do have an intended result that you work towards. However, whether that actually happens or not, is something you shouldn't ponder upon.

For example, in Mahabharata, Arjuna had to fight the war, plan his strategies keeping *Pandava* victory in mind. But whether they actually win the war or not, is not something Arjuna should worry about. Because fighting for justice was his duty but the resultant victory was not in his hands.

Once a goal is fixed in your mind, then bring your mind to the present and fix it on the process. Give it your full attention. Experience it fully. The process itself is full of little steps, all leading to the final end. Concentrate on achieving each step in the best way you can and with your complete effort or attention. This is what is meant by *'being in the present.'* This way you enjoy and experience the process fully even before you reach your goal. The final fruition eventually becomes all the more sweeter with a feeling of happiness, of a job thoroughly enjoyed and completed successfully.

More often than not, the satisfaction from the goal reached lasts for just a moment in time. Then the goal posts shift and another goal comes up to entice you. And so, it goes on. If your mind is on the end all the time, then you miss the process. *This means you miss your entire life in looking at the horizon.*

The end may not be what you desired. Rewards or acknowledgement may be wanting. But if you have enjoyed/experienced the process and given it your 100% then you have already retrieved most of the satisfaction from it. The feeling of disappointment when the end is not what you wanted is minimal or nil.

Going further in this chapter, we will discuss three broad processes to achieve success and fulfilment in our lives, the way the Gita has taught us. These include:

1. Focusing on the Process, not the Outcomes
2. The Role of Resilience in Strategic Planning
3. Managing Expectations in Uncertain Environments

Focusing on the Process, Not the Outcomes

If you have put your heart and soul into a project and found that the end product isn't what you hoped for, that's when you usually feel frustrated, disappointed or even question your abilities.

But what if there was another way to work?

What if instead of worrying about the outcome, you could be fully present in the process?

This is what Karma Yoga from the Bhagavad Gita teaches us, and it has lots to say about how we think about strategy, bounce back from problems, and lead others.

In the Gita, Lord Krishna tells Arjun to work without wanting the results of his actions. Krishna makes this point clear: we can control what we do, but not what happens after. This is really important in today's world, which changes rapidly and isn't very predictable.

Another shloka from the Gita says:

"Yogasthah kuru karmani sangam tyaktva dhananjaya siddhy-asiddhyoh samo bhutva samatvam yoga ucyate"

योगस्थो कुरु कर्माणि सङ्गं त्यक्त्वा धनञ्जय।
सिद्ध्यसिद्ध्योः समो भूत्वा समत्वं योग उच्यते॥

Do your work with a steady mind, giving up attachment, and be the same in success and failure. This balance is called yoga.

Whether you're a manager, business owner, or just dealing with your own problems, not focusing on results lets you pay attention to what really matters – doing your work well. This doesn't mean you don't care or have no goals. It means shifting focus from outside rewards to the good feeling of doing something well. This frees you from the ups and downs of success and failure and gives you a clear purpose for your choices.

When we focus on the process and not the outcome, it results in several benefits:

Less Worry

We live in a world obsessed with results. It's easy to get caught up in constantly thinking "*what if*" or "*what's next*". This creates a lot of stress and makes it hard to work well. But when we focus on the steps we can control, we feel calmer and can think more clearly.

Think about an artist starting a new painting. If they keep wondering *"Will this sell?"* or *"Will people like it?"* they might freeze up and struggle to create. But when they just enjoy mixing colours and trying different techniques, they get into a flow where painting itself becomes rewarding, regardless of what others think.

This works for everyone – be it running a business, studying for a test, or handling everyday problems. By focusing on what you can control, your effort and care, you escape the worry cycle. Your mind stays in the present, helping you work better and handle risks more calmly.

Better Work

When all your attention goes to the task instead of the outcome, you naturally do better work. We don't work as well when we're worried about success or failure. Always thinking about results creates a mental burden that distracts us and uses up energy. But when we stop worrying about outcomes, we give our best to the work and stay present.

A shloka in the Gita tells us:

"Buddhiyukto jahatiha ubhe sukrita-dushkrite tasmad yogaya yujyasva yogah karmasu kaushalam"

बुद्धियुक्तो जहाति ह उभे सुखृतदुष्कृते।
तस्माद्योगाय युज्यस्व योग: कर्मसु कौशलम्॥

A wise person leaves behind both good and bad results in this life itself. Therefore, commit yourself to yoga. Yoga is skill in action.

Picture a marathon runner who's focused completely on finishing the race or breaking her record. She might push too hard, doubt her pace, or stop when she shouldn't. But when she just focuses on keeping her rhythm, being aware of her body, and staying in the moment, she runs better. All her energy goes into running, not worrying about the finish line.

This applies to everyday life too. Someone preparing a presentation might worry so much about how people will receive it that they rush on the proper preparation. But they'll give a better presentation by simply focusing on creating good content and practicing well. When we're not preoccupied with what might happen, preparation becomes easier.

When we focus on the process, we become more careful, more creative, and more interested in the work itself. Better results often follow naturally, not because we were chasing them, but because we were fully involved in what we were doing.

More Learning

One of the best things about detachment is seeing outcomes as feedback instead of judgment. When we step back from expected results, we can view success and failure the same way: *As chances to learn.* This makes every experience positive because it helps us grow and improve.

Consider someone launching a new product. If they're focused only on sales targets, falling short feels like a personal failure. This discouragement might make them afraid to take risks in the future. But if they can detach from outcomes, they are able to see the situation more clearly. They might uncover useful insights. Maybe customers noticed design problems, or the marketing targeted the wrong people. What looked like a failure can actually be helpful feedback for making things better.

This mindset helps in personal relationships too. In disagreements, not being attached to "*winning*" the argument lets us focus on understanding each other and communicating better. It's not about who wins, but how the relationship improves.

Detachment helps us make decisions without fear of judgment and learn from results. Every setback becomes preparation for the next attempt, and every success becomes a foundation for the next effort. This changes how we approach problems and opportunities, making growth ongoing.

The Role of Resilience in Strategic Planning

This principle helps us focus on things we can control, such as our actions and decisions, rather than things we can't. Think of a chess player who plans several moves ahead but knows the game's outcome remains uncertain. Instead of obsessing over winning, the resilient player adapts their strategy as the game unfolds, staying calm and flexible.

In strategic planning, nothing is certain. Markets change, competitors emerge, and surprises happen. The resilient leader addresses these uncertainties with a clear mind that allows for adaptable responses.

A shloka from the Gita says:

"Sukha-duhkhe same kritva labhalabhau jayajayau tato yuddhaya yujyasva naivam papam avapsyasi"

सुखदु:खेसमं कृत्वा लाभालाभौ जयजयौ।
ततो युद्धाय युज्यस्व नैवं पापमवाप्स्यसि॥

Treat happiness and sadness, gain and loss, victory and defeat the same. Then prepare for battle, and you will not incur sin.

Staying True to Purpose

Good strategists connect their actions to a larger purpose, just as Krishna told Arjuna to work according to his dharma. A clear purpose acts like a compass, guiding decisions and actions with certainty even when things are uncertain.

This purpose keeps you steady during tough times. Every journey has problems, losses, and failures. But when we see these as temporary challenges rather than defining events, we keep moving forward.

This is what Krishna taught Arjuna: *Knowing your duty lets you act with confidence regardless of what's happening around you.*

In business strategy, staying grounded means directing all actions toward a shared vision. A manager launching a new product might face unexpected problems. Focusing on short-term results, like sales figures could lead to discouragement. But if their efforts connect to a higher purpose, such as serving customers or creating innovation, they find motivation to adjust strategies and overcome obstacles.

Purpose-driven action builds resilience and motivates teams. People who understand what they're doing and why they're doing it stick together through hard times. Ultimately, purpose turns setbacks into learning opportunities that lead to real growth and success.

Seeing Challenges as Opportunities

Detachment teaches us not to see failures as dead ends but as steps in learning. Every setback becomes a chance to adjust tactics, revise plans, and build character. Krishna explains how to work without worrying about consequences, showing that failure isn't final. It's just another step toward success.

Imagine a company launching a product that gets negative feedback. If the company takes this as a failure, they might lose confidence or abandon the project. But with detachment, they can see customer input as valuable information. They can analyse reactions objectively, make changes, and improve the product. Often, this adjustment process leads to greater success than would have been possible without the initial problems.

This requires seeing every experience, good or bad, as contributing to growth. This mindset helps people and teams stay positive even in difficult times. An entrepreneur whose first business fails might learn crucial lessons about markets, finance, or leadership that prove invaluable later.

When viewed as opportunities, problems reveal potential solutions. People facing obstacles become more willing to try new approaches and adapt to changing circumstances. This frees us to focus on continuous improvement rather than short-term results.

Balancing Flexibility and Persistence

Resilience requires knowing when to change direction and when to keep going. The detached mindset of Karma Yoga allows for clear decisions by removing personal biases about what outcomes should be.

Another teaching from the Gita says:

"Uddhared atmanatmanam natmanam avasadayet atmaiva hy atmano bandhur atmaiva ripur atmanah"

उद्धरेत् आत्मनात्मानं नात्मानमवसादयेत्।
आत्मैव ह्यात्मनो बन्धुरात्मैव रिपुरात्मनः॥

Lift yourself up by yourself; don't put yourself down. Your mind alone can be your friend, and your mind alone can be your enemy.

When we're too invested in outcomes, fear of failure can cloud our judgment. We might stick with plans that aren't working or abandon promising approaches too quickly. A detached mind enables decision-making without emotional bias. It considers current conditions rather than desired outcomes or past investments.

Consider a start-up that isn't getting the expected market response. A flexible, detached mindset would allow the team to adapt — perhaps repositioning their offering or modifying features, without seeing the initial results as failure. Detachment helps navigate challenges while keeping sight of long-term goals.

This balance also involves managing emotions. Failures can discourage us, while small successes might make us complacent. Detachment helps maintain consistency, preventing frustration or overconfidence from interfering with the process.

The long-term benefit is adaptability with direction. Strategies change as environments evolve, while goals remain in focus. These complementary forces form the foundation of resilience and effective planning.

Managing Expectations in Uncertain Environments

Uncertainty is a part of life and strategy. Volatile markets, unexpected technological changes, and unforeseen events mean that leaders often face situations without guarantees. Managing expectations in such environments is crucial, and Karma Yoga offers valuable insights.

Krishna's main teaching to Arjuna is to do his duty without worrying about success or failure. This wisdom helps us navigate uncertainty without swinging between arrogance and despair.

Setting Realistic Expectations

Ambition drives progress, but unrealistic expectations can create frustration, doubt, and burnout. Karma Yoga suggests setting goals that acknowledge what's within our control, such as our efforts, while recognizing that external factors influence outcomes.

Setting realistic expectations isn't settling for less, it's creating achievable goals. A team launching a new product might want market leadership. Rather than expecting immediate success, they could establish specific targets: *gathering customer feedback, achieving steady sales growth, and refining the product.* This allows them to measure progress while adjusting to challenges.

A shloka reminds us:

"Prajahati yada kaman sarvan partha manogatan atmany evatmana tushtah sthita-prajna tada ucyate"

प्रजाहति यदा कामान्सर्वान्पार्थ मनोगतान्।
आत्मन्येवात्मना तुष्टः स्थितप्रज्ञः तदा उच्यते॥

When a person gives up all desires of the mind and finds satisfaction in the self alone, then they are said to be steady in wisdom.

Detachment helps us recognize that despite careful planning, unexpected factors will affect results as everything cannot be forseen. Things like economic changes and/or new competition may impact outcomes. Acknowledging these possibilities reduces disappointment when setbacks occur.

This mindset creates an environment where everyone stays motivated, accepts setbacks as part of the process, and adjusts goals as needed. It builds resilience that sustains the pursuit of ambitious goals without being derailed by rigid expectations.

Communicating Clearly

In uncertain situations, honest communication builds trust. When people don't understand challenges and risks, they often create their own explanations, leading to misunderstandings. Transparency increases awareness and promotes collaboration.

Honest communication means clearly stating what is 'known' and 'unknown'. A project manager might tell their team, "*We have a good plan, but there are risks like supply problems or resource limits. We're working to reduce these risks, but delays are possible.*" This sets proper expectations, builds trust, and prepares everyone for potential challenges.

Open communication also fosters partnership. Sharing challenges invites others to contribute ideas and solutions, encouraging teamwork. This might mean sharing information across departments to find the best solution to a problem.

Rather than undermining confidence, transparency enhances it. When teams understand potential obstacles, they're more likely to support the process.

Focusing on What You Can Control

Krishna's advice to act without worrying about results applies perfectly to our modern world, where many factors lie beyond our control. This perspective channels our energy toward elements we can influence, making us more effective and calm.

A shloka in the Gita teaches:

"Karmendriyani samyamya ya aste manasa smaran indriyarthan vimudhatma mithyacarah sa ucyate"

कर्मेन्द्रियाणि संयम्य या अस्ते मनसा स्मरन्।
इन्द्रियार्थान्विमूढात्मा मिथ्याचारः स उच्यते॥

One who restrains the senses but whose mind dwells on sense objects certainly deludes himself and is called a pretender.

Practical leadership means identifying tasks and decisions within your control. Instead of worrying whether a product will succeed in the market, a business leader can focus on improving the product, researching the market, and engaging with customers. Similarly, job seekers in competitive markets can concentrate on creating good resumes, networking, and preparing for interviews rather than complaining about the state of the job market.

This approach includes continuous improvement. Working on controllable factors like refining processes, developing skills, and building relationships creates a foundation for future success. These seemingly small efforts become daily investments that help navigate uncertainties and opportunities.

Focusing on what you can control transforms your mindset from powerlessness to empowerment. It enables practical action in the present moment, embodying the spirit of detachment for clear thinking amid uncertainty.

Conclusion

The teaching of detachment from outcomes is central to the Bhagavad Gita. It forms the core of dharma ethics, providing wisdom for overcoming life's challenges and finding right solutions. This approach shifts attention from external results to the quality of our actions, making process the focus. Through this practice, we develop confidence, clarity, and purpose.

Krishna's message reveals that true fulfilment comes not from external achievements but from the sincerity in our actions. Whether in leadership, personal development, or decision-making, practicing detachment frees us from unnecessary burdens, allowing us to contribute with wholeness.

As a final teaching of this chapter, the Gita tells us:

"Sarva-dharman parityajya mam ekam sharanam vraja aham tvam sarva-papebhyo mokshayishyami ma shucah"

सर्वधर्मान्परित्यज्य मामेकं शरणं व्रज।
अहं त्वां सर्वपापेभ्यो मोक्षयिष्यामि मा शुचः॥

Abandon all kinds of duties and just surrender to me. I will deliver you from all sinful reactions. Do not fear.

This approach sharpens our problem-solving abilities with focus and creativity. By releasing attachment to success and failure, we awaken our rational and adaptive capabilities. We gain the power to use time and energy constructively, creating a future aligned with our values.

Krishna's advice to Arjuna of steadiness in action regardless of results, offers the right perspective. Through this lens, we gain not just a tool for strategic thinking but a path toward fulfilling life's purpose. When we approach challenges with awareness of both our own needs and others' values, we create the conditions for everyone to thrive.

The strategies we've explored show us that the process itself is the medium for growth. This mindset aligns our approach with structures that support progress, building resilience and enabling evolution. When we engage fully in the process with clarity and commitment, the desired outcomes often follow. This happens not because we grasped for results, but because we honoured the journey.

CHAPTER 3

Adaptability (Jnana Yoga)

The ability to adapt, a strategist should know, is of vital importance in today's fast-changing world. In the Bhagavad Gita, Jnana Yoga is the way to go in knowing about knowledge, learning, and flexibility in dealing with life's uncertainties.

Change is the only thing that is unchanging in the personal as well as the professional sphere of life. There are people who do not like it because of the fear or attachment to it. But at the same time those who accept it can change their problems into their own advantage. The Bhagavad Gita reaffirms that the earth is in a cycle that propagates the world. Day follows night, seasons shift, and new possibilities emerge as old ones fade away. Knowing this natural rhythm allows us to deal with change in a better way than fighting against it.

A powerful shloka in the Gita says:

"Vasamsi jirnani yatha vihaya navani grhnati naro 'parani tatha sarirani vihaya jirnany anyani samyati navani dehi"

वसांसि जिर्नानि यथा विहाय नवानि ग्रिह्णाति नारोऽपराणि।
तथा शरीराणि विहाय जिर्नान्यिन्यानी सम्यति नवानि देही॥

Just as a person puts on new garments, giving up old ones, the soul similarly accepts new material bodies giving up the old and useless ones.

Jnana Yoga, also known as the Path of Knowledge guides one towards wisdom, judgment, and a deeper sense of reality. It is based on the belief that knowledge is not something fixed, but is rather made up of a series of constant changes. Just like a river that carves and shapes its path, we, as human beings, should be adaptable, flexible and develop innovative and smarter solutions in our minds.

Adaptability has nothing to do with merely responding to the changes; it implies staying ahead of changes. A genuine leader is not someone who waits for things to happen first then pick out the best option, rather they are the ones who go out there and find the knowledge needed to predict future challenges. Quite simply, it involves collecting information from the past, being mindful of the latest fashion, and preparing for unexpected events. The ability to learn, unlearn, and relearn is the basic principle of Jnana Yoga.

Strategic adaptability also underlines the importance of letting go of specific goals. Krishna is counselling Arjuna in the explication of the Gita to focus on his duties manfully while not to be attached to the end result. This means not to act without cause, but to see the whole picture and to be adaptive in achieving the goal. A leader that is very committed to a single blueprint is at risk of miscalculations when circumstances change. On the contrary, winning leaders are unwavering adherents of their paramount values while at the same time they are flexible enough to change their tactics when necessary.

This chapter examines the way Jnana Yoga's principles can be applied to strategic thinking and leadership. We will discuss how to not shy away from change, how to embrace a learning mindset and how to become more strategic and flexible in our approach. Leadership that leverages these perceptions is breaking their way to the top of the mountain; it is part of the trials and tribulations of the human condition, what was once a seamless life becoming a roller coaster of milestones. Leaders will become successful only when they see the unknown as a place where they can grow. They will become winners.

Embracing Change and New Insights

Change is inevitable. In the Bhagavad Gita, Krishna reveals to Arjuna the eternal nature of the soul and the temporary nature of the body, teaching him to embrace change rather than fear it.

Another beautiful shloka from the Gita tells us:

"Jatasya hi dhruvo mrtyur dhruvam janma mrtasya ca tasmad apariharye 'rthe na tvam socitum arhasi"

जातस्य हि ध्रुवो मृत्युरध्रुवं जन्म मृतस्य च।
तस्मादपरिहार्येऽर्थे न त्वं शोकितुमर्हसि।।

For one who has taken birth, death is certain, and for one who is dead, birth is certain. Therefore, you should not lament over the inevitable.

This verse reminds us that change is the natural order of things. What comes must go and what goes must come again in some form. This wisdom applies not just to life and death, but to all aspects of existence including our strategies, plans, and approaches to challenges.

Why Adaptability Matters

Those who do not adapt become outdated, and those who welcome change become better. For instance, let us look at the Nokia and Kodak companies. They were once the biggest companies in their industries but could not adjust to the new trends: *Nokia to the smart phone revolution and Kodak to digital photography.*

On the other hand, companies such as Apple and Amazon continuously reinvent themselves, thus remaining current through taking the course of adaptation.

How to Embrace Change Strategically

1. Develop a Growth Mindset

Consider that change could be an event in your life where you could grow as a person rather than the opposite. Try to stay open to learning new things and to new experiences. Having a growth mindset means that problems are seen as the ladders to climb up and become better instead of the walls that stop you. The more important idea is to take risks and to fail with the right attitude, knowing that each mistake is a part of the learning process.

The Gita reminds us:

"Na hi jnanena sadrsam pavitram iha vidyate tat svayam yoga-samsiddhah kalenatmani vindati"

न हि ज्ञानेन सदृशं पवित्रं इह विद्यते।
तत्स्वयं योगसंशुद्धः कालेनात्मनि विन्दति॥

In this world, there is nothing as pure as knowledge. One who has become perfect in yoga finds this knowledge within himself in due course of time.

A person who has a growth mindset believes that their knowledge and intelligence can be improved and developed with time, effort, and staying power. Using curiosity and the ability to change to our side will make for a happy life. Ask for advice and take learning of the lessons received from the mistakes as the main teaching. Also, always look for methods to improve. Be proactive while looking for new knowledge and skills that fit in with changing circumstances. Through the practice of adaptability and persistence, both people and organizations can survive in the unknown and convert setbacks into opportunities for creativity and success.

2. Anticipate Change

Establish connections, get to know the customers' usual way of acting and understand about the new technology. Prediction of change makes the team become the precedent rather than the instruments that will only be troubled by the disruption. Companies can initially become agile and pivot by simply keeping an eye on and rapidly implementing the shifting trends in the industry and early-stage innovation which prompts digital alteration.

Krishna teaches Arjuna:

"Prakrteh kriyamanani gunaih karmani sarvasah ahankara-vimudhatma kartaham iti manyate"

प्रकृतैः क्रियमाणानि गुणैः कर्माणि सर्वशः।
आहंकारविमूढात्मा कर्ताहमिति मन्यते॥

All activities are carried out by the three modes of material nature. But in ignorance, the soul, deluded by false identification with the body, thinks itself to be the doer.

This implies interpreting and visualizing data for decision-making, intently watching for competitors and quickly identifying any impetus for change. Good leaders achieve insight through interacting with authorities, participating in ventures and updating their expertise. They should look at change as a moment to regenerate and to surpass their competitors. Companies see this as a way to prepare for the future with a long-term vision, while the world is becoming more dynamic and unpredictable.

3. Be Willing to Let Go

Refusing to let go of outdated strategies or ideas may actually slow down progress. Knowing when to embrace change marks a crucial leadership skill. To be able to change requires self-awareness coupled with a bravery to look back honestly, to throw away the "*I am right*" or bad feelings that you may usually attach to the decision you made.

As Krishna advises:

"Niyatam kuru karma tvam karma jyayo hy akarmanah sarira-yatrapi ca te na prasiddhyed akarmanah"

नियतं कुरु कर्म त्वं कर्म ज्यायो ह्यकर्मणः।
शरीरयात्रापि च ते न प्रसिद्ध्येद अकर्मणः॥

Perform your prescribed duty, for action is better than inaction. A man cannot even maintain his physical body without work.

A strategy that has worked for years may not be useful today and holding fast to the old methods can only hamper the progress. However, instead of persisting with the old ways despite the changes in technology and the capability of one's organization, one should adapt to change and continuously monitor the performance and gather the feedback from more people.

4. Encourage Experimentation

It is important to let people think creatively and innovate in your company. Inventing ideas encourages the creativity that leads to the constant development of the organization's work. Executives need to create an environment in which the employees not only face challenges but also are willing to take risks. Small experiments can be carried out to integrate the fresh point of view, while the rest of the team members discuss and come up with the main project ideas.

The wisdom of the Gita tells us:

"Saktah karmany avidvamso yatha kurvanti bharata kuryad vidvams tathasaktah cikirsur loka-sangraham"

सक्तः कर्माणि अविद्वांसो यथा कुर्वन्ति भारत।
कुर्याद् विद्वांस् तथा सक्तः चिकीर्षुर् लोकसंग्रहम्॥

As the ignorant perform their duties with attachment, O descendant of Bharata, so the wise should act without attachment, for the welfare of the world.

By giving rewards for the risk-taking and being open to the lessons learned from the errors, the organization can move towards the culture of innovation. Experiments that lead to breakthroughs can create products that give the organisation a competitive edge in the market over time. Availing benefits from the strategies of trial-and-error, companies which thrive on the mindset that setbacks are necessary for real progress and change are the most outstanding companies today.

One way to ensure that we can last and be more resilient is to cultivate our capacity to welcome and adapt the change.

Developing a Learning Organization

Krishna stresses in the Gita the importance of knowledge and wisdom:

"Sreyān dravyamayād yajñāj jñānayajñah parantapa sarvam karmākhilam pārtha jñāne parisamāpyate"

श्रेयान् द्रव्यमयाद्यज्ञात् ज्ञानयज्ञः परंतप।
सर्वं कर्माखिलं पार्थ ज्ञानें परिसमाप्यते॥

Better than the sacrifice of material possessions is the sacrifice of knowledge, O scorcher of foes. For all actions without exception culminate in knowledge.

A learning organization is a permanently open system about developing insights, gaining knowledge, and applying it in practice. In a world that is evolving so rapidly, it doesn't take long for traditional knowledge to become obsolete. The main cause is the necessity of the development of the skill of learning how to learn in the organizations and individuals.

What is a Learning Organization?

A learning organization is an organization in which the culture is so embedded with the information-sharing, creativity, and adaptability that the people there habitually question the existing methods, come up with new ideas, and improve continuously. The previous statement is credited by such establishments, which give the staff the green light to be creative in solving existing problems.

Characteristics of a Learning Organization

1. Encourages Continuous Learning

Keeping up the learning process not only helps the leaders and the employees, but also the organizations themselves to remain flexible in the fast pace of the world that is constantly changing. The art of lifelong learning is an imperative survival skill in this ever-evolving dynamic world that we live in. Learning new things is important, and if one does not follow the industry's trend, he or she will be left behind. The need for training never ends; the competitive workplace nature continuously demands the development of skills.

The Gita encourages seeking knowledge:

"Ahaṁ sarvasya prabhavo mattaḥ sarvaṁ pravartate iti matvā bhajante māṁ budhā bhāva-samanvitāḥ"

अहं सर्वस्य प्रभवो मत्तः सर्वं प्रवर्तते।

इति मत्वा भजंते मां बुद्धा भावसमन्विताः॥

I am the source of all spiritual and material worlds. Everything emanates from Me. The wise who perfectly know this engage in My devotional service and worship Me with all their hearts.

2. Creates a Culture of Knowledge Sharing

Teams must share what they know. Together, we can solve more problems. New ideas come from open discussions. Together, we can come up with new ideas. Then, our team becomes better able to deal with change. Being open at work helps people learn from one another. So, make places where exchange of information can take place. A good leader listens to everyone. If we share ideas, we can face any future challenges.

3. Embraces Failure as a Learning Opportunity

Errors help to improve. By failing, you learn more and become better. When mistakes happen, you check what went wrong and fix it as a team. If it's okay to try new things, then you can stumble upon new ways.

Krishna teaches in the Gita:

"Durena hy avaram karma buddhi-yogad dhananjaya buddhau sharanam anviccha kripanah phala-hetavah"

दूरें हि अवरं कर्म बुद्धियोगाद्धनञ्जय।
बुद्धौ शरणमांविच्छ क्रिपाणः फलहेतवः॥

Intelligence is far better than unintelligent work. Seek refuge in intelligence, O Arjuna. Pitiable are those who work only for rewards.

Organizations grow when novelty is encouraged. By learning from failing, people and companies become stronger.

4. Invests in Training and Development

Companies should provide employees with resources for learning and opportunities for growth. A company that invests in training and development will have employees who constantly improve their skills, be well-versed with the industry's trend, and be flexible in the face of development. Workshops, mentorship programs, online courses, and leadership training are some of the options here. Increased professional growth support among employees is directly proportional to their productivity, engagement, and innovation. Apart from the employees, the organization is also a stakeholder due to a knowledgeable and resilient workforce supported by lifelong learning which not only adds value for individuals but also makes organizational culture stronger by helping the organization to cope with the ever-changing challenges that the market is presenting.

5. Values Curiosity and Inquiry

The staff need to question things. When curiosity is valued, new ideas and improvements happen. We need to look for better ways and think outside the box. Leaders should listen to employees and let their teams experiment.

This verse emphasizes:

"Yasmin jñāte sarvam idaṁ jñātaṁ bhavati ekaṁ vijñāya sarvaṁ vijñātaṁ bhavati"

यस्मिन्ज्ञाते सर्वमिदं ज्ञातं भवति एकं विज्ञाय सर्वं विज्ञातं भवति।

By knowing which, everything is known; by understanding one, everything is understood.

When we share and talk openly, it develops our thinking and problem solving. Being open-minded helps companies adapt to changes in the world.

Examples of Learning Organizations

- Google promotes staff by reserving time off to be used to the extent of 20% of their time which they can use to work on innovative projects that go beyond the scope of their tasks. This practice has resulted in the discovery of such apps as email and maps for Google.
- The fundamental principle of Kaizen that Toyota adheres is continuous improvement, a philosophy focused on making small, incremental changes over

time to achieve significant results. It emphasizes a proactive approach to identifying and resolving issues, rather than waiting for problems to escalate.

- It is a principle of quality. Employees at all levels are encouraged to think of new ways to address the challenges they face.

Strategic Flexibility and Dynamic Decision-Making

Krishna clarifies to Arjuna about the need to perform one's duty along with detachment from the results of the task:

"Yogasthah kuru karmani sangam tyaktva dhananjaya siddhyasiddhyoh samo bhutva samatvam yoga ucyate"

योगस्थो कुरु कर्माणि सङ्गं त्यक्त्वा धनञ्जय।
सिद्ध्यसिद्ध्योः समो भूत्वा समत्वं योग उच्यते॥

Perform your duty equipoised, O Arjuna, abandoning all attachment to success or failure. Such equanimity is called yoga.

The stated policy is about strategic flexibility which is the opposite of the ability to focus on doing something and to open up to the necessary adjustments throughout.

Why Strategic Flexibility is Crucial

When operating in any business environment, the unpredictable nature of the enterprise is evident, mostly whether you are an old-hand or a young entrepreneur. In the midst of the changes and surprises, many strict plans fail outright because they are based on the assumption that the tomorrow will be the same as today. However, a true leader is someone that can effectively plan for the unknown.

Principles of Strategic Flexibility

1. Be Prepared for Multiple Scenarios

Working on a single operation can be a great solution, but if we are slightly open-minded, we may think about different conditions for the current event. Organizations could fail to meet probable event details and make up for them in the future by making a better plan that visualizes these events and forms a means of a probable response.

Krishna teaches:

"Buddhau saranam anviccha kripanah phala-hetavah"

बुद्धौ शरणमांविच्छ क्रिपाणः फलहेतवः।

Seek refuge in intelligence. Pitiable are those who work only for rewards.

This type of forward thinking presents numerous options when it comes to running various operations as you will have the ability to respond adequately at any time if the need arises. On the basis of the proactive foresight, those who espouse this approach are seen to perform the handling of elements and the minimizing of risks and that they will always have a competitive advantage as they are ready for change and challenge in any given complex globe.

2. Monitor Key Indicators

In case questions like the business environment's changes are to be answered, the best way to do it is to intensively keep under constant review not only specific indicators of various branches in the industry but also global economy changes. In the quite-shifting marketplace, companies maximize their gains by thoroughly monitoring the feedback circle among the client, the competition's methodologies, and the financial metrics.

3. Encourage Decentralized Decision-Making

Preventing sales slides and revenue crashes will be easier if a business is aware of the environment conditions with the use of key performance indicators, industry trends, and economic shifts. Companies can distinguish between potential risks and opportunities by looking at customer feedback data, the strategies their competitors follow, and their own financial metrics.

A powerful teaching from the Gita:

"Yatha prakasayaty ekah krtsnam lokam imam ravih ksetram ksetri tatha krtsnam prakasayati bharata"

यथा प्रकाशयत्येकः कृत्स्नं लोकमिमं रविः।
क्षेत्रं क्षेत्री तथा कृत्स्नं प्रकाशयति भारत॥

As the sun alone illuminates all this universe, so does the living entity, one within the body, illuminate the entire body by consciousness.

The company may have a trend of making decisions due to data-driven forecasts, and this will enable the management to remain competitive in the evolving marketplace. The best decision is to analyse customer feedback, competitor strategies, and financial metrics.

4. Balance Commitment and Agility

Putting all your effort into achieving long-term goals while being ready to change tactics due to circumstances is an approach that should be followed in order to accomplish your ultimate objectives. The most effective leaders are those who have a fixed and clear goal with the ability to adapt themselves to new conditions. This equilibrium hinges on reviewing progress continuously, seeking thoughts from others, and being agile to deviate when needed. Amidst a changing world, the organizations that learn it will continue to be resilient, creative, and responsive.

Examples of Strategic Flexibility

- Netflix: The concept behind Netflix was quite simple; it all started as a firm that would give people an opportunity to rent movies conveniently. It was the service that would allow for DVD rental through mail on a monthly rental basis but soon the firm changed course due to the massive growth in the digital consumption especially with speedy and smooth access to the internet.

- Tesla: Evolving its robust capabilities and establishments in technology and production processes, the company continuously improves them ensuring it stays ahead of its competitors.

Conclusion

The knowledge expressed through action, as portrayed in the yoga of knowledge, teaches that adaptability involves educating oneself, staying up to date, and being strategically flexible.

If growth is the orientation instead of the resistance due to the fact that change is natural, then we derive positive benefits from it.

Be the one who brings about a learning organization and obtains a context in which change is not difficult but an automatic thing for all workers, because we create conditions for our company to always be on the crest of a wave.

As a final teaching, the Gita tells us:

"Yadrccha-labha-santusto dvandvatito vimatsarah samah siddhav asiddhau ca krtvapi na nibadhyate"

यदृच्छालाभसन्तुष्टो द्वन्द्वातीतो विमत्सरः।
समः सिद्धावसिद्धौ च कृत्वापि न निवद्यते॥

Content with gain that comes of its own accord, free from duality and envy, steady in both success and failure, one is never entangled, even while performing actions.

The wisdom of the Bhagavad Gita is unchangeable and its teachings of ability to change remain the same today as they were a few thousand years ago. Leaders who possess the qualities of adaptability, just like Arjuna, who overcame doubts and addressed challenges with wisdom, will successfully manage the intricacies of the modern world.

In a time of great instability, those who are open to change will not only survive but also grow. The leaders who are flexible and yet at the same time maintain their core values are in the best position to make good decisions even when the future is unknown. Through the process of continuous learning, adaptation of strategies, and building an innovative culture, individuals and companies can change the scenario in their favour. And what if during your next episode of uncertainty you take Krishna's advice? Act it out with wisdom, openness, and trust. By following this, you will not be just a better decision-maker but a stronger and more awakened leader, who is able to turn challenges into opportunities and also lead the others towards success.

CHAPTER 4

Leadership And Delegation (Karma Sannyasa Yoga)

Good leaders guide, inspire, and empower people. In the Bhagavad Gita, Krishna talks about Karma Yoga and Sannyasa Yoga. These ideas show us how leaders must balance responsibility and detachment while still enabling others to work confidently and clearly.

A leader must care more about others' success more than their own power. One does not push to get ahead but uses their power for creating a collaborative environment. Krishna guides Arjuna to act without getting caught up in the results. Similarly, leaders must make wise decisions based on duty, not their egos.

A beautiful shloka in the Gita illustrates this wisdom:

"Na kartritvam na karmani lokasya srijati prabhuh na karma phala samyogam svabhavastu pravartate"

न कर्तृत्वं न कर्माणि लोकस्य सृजति प्रभुः।
न कर्मफलसंयोगं स्वभावस्तु प्रवर्तते॥

The Lord neither creates the sense of doer-ship nor the actions of people, nor the connection with the fruits of actions. These all happen naturally.

There is a fine line between using one's authority and trusting others. A leader should not control everything but inspire those they are leading. They need to delegate duties while providing guidance and oversight. Krishna leads by giving advice, not ruling; so, should modern leaders by offering direction and autonomy.

Delegation is a huge part of leadership. It doesn't mean passing the buck; rather, it is ensuring that the right person does the job they can do well. Not letting go of control means leaders have no time to think. To delegate well, choose the right people, make expectations clear and build trust and accountability.

This chapter considers delegation, empowering employees, and aligning strategy with actual execution. Leaders who adopt these concepts promote teamwork that is innovative and persistently successful, just as Krishna encouraged Arjuna with knowledge.

Delegating Effectively for Strategic Focus

Understanding Delegation as a Strategic Tool

Good leaders know that they cannot do everything. They have to prioritize and delegate. Bhagavad Gita says leaders should not worry about the results of their duties. This philosophy advises leaders to trust their team to complete tasks on their own.

As the Gita teaches:

"Yogasthah kuru karmani sangam tyaktva dhananjaya siddhyasiddhyoh samo bhutva samatvam yoga ucyate"

योगस्थो कुरु कर्माणि सङ्गं त्यक्त्वा धनञ्जय।
सिद्ध्यसिद्ध्योः समो भूत्वा समत्वं योग उच्यते॥

Perform your duties with equanimity, O Arjuna, abandoning attachment to success or failure. Such equanimity is called yoga.

Delegating wisely helps to make teams stronger. Leaders must identify which tasks are their top priorities. They need to choose suitable people to take on other tasks. Clear guidance and support are important for a smooth delegation process. Success metrics and strengths alignment are also vital.

Micromanaging is something leaders must avoid. Support when needed is the better approach. Delegating eases the workload for leaders. It empowers staff. They can develop skills and make contributions as well.

The Art of Letting Go

Leaders nowadays are afraid to delegate. They tend to oversee everything they do and every decision they make. But they need to know that not everything depends on them and those around can still take care of themselves.

Krishna conveys this wisdom to Arjuna:

"Karmanye vadhikaraste ma phaleshu kadachana ma karma phala hetur bhurma te sangostva karmani"

कर्मण्येवाधिकारस्ते मा फलेषु कदाचन।
मा कर्मफलहेतुर्भूर्मा ते सङ्गोऽस्त्वकर्मणि॥

You have a right to perform your duty, but the results are not dependent on you. Never consider yourself to be the cause of the results, and never be attached to inaction.

It's tough to let go. Real leaders know that they can't control every little thing. When you give the members of your team more freedom to think about the way they do the task rather than the features of the job itself, they become more committed to what they do.

It is true that errors provide a great opportunity for learning and development. Employees are supposed to think independently, make choices, and take risks. Recognition that the seeking of continuous improvement is based on the acceptance of mistakes as well.

Leaders can delegate allowing the team to develop independently. This eases the pressure and the staff can concentrate on their own roles. Over time this offers a team great capacity in case leaders retire.

Identifying What to Delegate

Not all decisions with small long-term impacts are to be postponed. Among the things that require human intervention, leaders should leave the jobs with the highest impact, including core strategic initiatives and tasks that are closely connected with their personal expertise.

The delegation of the routine activities, administrative work, and technical execution should be given to the team members who are capable. The Eisenhower Matrix, which is used to place tasks into compartments based on their urgency and importance, is a useful tool that helps determine what can be delegated.

Being careful with delegation enables the leaders to capitalize on strategic decision-making, while feeding their subordinates with support for operational activities. Leaders are most successful when they assign duties that precisely match the talent, know-how, and growth aspirations of their people.

Furthermore, by transferring the responsibility of regular chores to others, the barren space of a leader's time gets filled with creative efforts and other innovations. Regular appraisals along with continuous feedback are the thrusts that keep the delegated duties tightly interconnected with the organizational goals while giving employees the assistance they require to succeed.

Empowering Teams through Leadership

Creating a Culture of Trust

Empowerment of the employees is the cornerstone of trust. Employee productivity is maximized by entrusting and appreciating them. A healthy work atmosphere, which allows employees to choose is the result of leaders who foster it. Krishna through his wisdom and clarity, helped Arjuna feel empowered, however it was still Arjuna's responsibility to make his own choices.

The Gita teaches us about the power of trust:

"Uddhared atmanatmanam natmanam avasadayet atmaiva hy atmano bandhur atmaiva ripur atmanah"

उद्धरेत् आत्मनात्मानं नात्मानमवसादयेत्।
आत्मैव ह्यात्मनो बन्धुरात्मैव रिपुरात्मनः॥

One must elevate oneself by one's own mind, not degrade oneself. The mind is the friend of the conditioned soul, and the mind is also its enemy.

Trust building within an organization begins with transparency. Leaders should share openly their plans, expectations, and the tasks that they face. Employees are more satisfied when they are informed about the direction the organization is taking because they will feel more connected to the broader vision of the company. The clearness of the process takes away questions, anxiety and increases the employees' self-confidence.

Encouraging autonomy is another essential factor when one talks about confidence-building through the own actions. Leaders have to let their staff decide about the things related to their work. Through micromanaging, creativity is suppressed which may also result in frustration and lack of confidence; on the contrary, giving employees the right to govern their work brings about a feeling of the responsibility and accountability to them.

Encouraging Ownership and Accountability

Leaders communicate well when tasking and they also create a feeling of belonging to the teams. Members who are given the responsibility for their given tasks are naturally most likely to be motivated and fully involved. Recognize and reward work appropriately. True ownership arises from feeling essential and deeply engaged in the task.

Krishna's wisdom reminds us:

"Tasmad asaktah satatam karyam karma samacara asakto hy acaran karma param apnoti purusah"

तस्मादसक्तः सततं कार्यं कर्म समाचर।
असक्तो ह्याचरन्कर्म परमाप्नोति पुरुषः॥

Therefore, without attachment, perform always the work that has to be done, for a person who performs work without attachment attains the Supreme.

One of first steps to taking ownership for workers is comprehending how their job impacts the company's achievements. This sense of belonging can be done when leaders are clear about the roles and responsibilities, have expectations and support decision-making among all on the team. By allowing staff to take the initiative, staff connects more deeply to their work and become emotionally invested in the accomplishment of positive results.

Accountability is one of the main functions of high performance. The heads need to set the measurable goals and bring the snap of the electrodes into the working quarters to make sure their employees are in the right track. The guiding beacons not only know the right direction but also clearly show the areas that need to be improved. Constructive feedback fostered by the supportive encouragement tightens up the sense of responsibility whilegiving room for creativity at the same time.

Providing Learning Opportunities

Empowerment means constant growth as well. Leaders that are interested in their team's skill set improvement should sponsor training, mentorship, and skill-building programs. It is not only performance that is affected by learning but this is also one way to prepare employees for more responsibilities in the future.

The Gita's wisdom emphasizes continual learning:

"Na hi jnanena sadrsam pavitram iha vidyate tat svayam yoga-samsiddhah kalenatmani vindati"

न हि ज्ञानेंन सदृशं पवित्रं इह विद्यते।

तत्स्वयं योगसंशुद्धः कालेनात्मनि विन्दति॥

There is nothing in this world as purifying as knowledge. In time, when one is perfected in yoga, one finds this knowledge within oneself.

It is great to know that learning is one of the essential parts of a company's culture. Managers can put their employees' development first by launching various structured training programs, on-the-job coaching, and mentorship projects. Options like industry-related courses, workshops, and certifications help teammates to be informed about the latest trends and technologies.

The inspiration of a growth mindset among staff members that can help them look at challenges as learning moments are important. Managers have to establish the right environment so that employees feel comfortable to try new things out, make risks with a plan, and grow from their mistakes. Cross-functional learning is a unique opportunity for a team member to build new skills and help them to have a much better scope of things in the organization.

Balancing High-Level Strategy and Tactical Execution

Maintaining Strategic Vision

For a good leader, it isn't only the future that one thinks about; living in the present is equally important. The operation of the business daily is undoubtedly important, but the broader vision should be no less prioritized. The strategic clarity that links all efforts with the long-term goals is very important.

Krishna shares this vision:

"Mayy arpita-mano-buddhir mam evaisyasy asamsayah"

मय्यर्पितमनोबुद्धिरममेवैश्यस्यसंशय:।

With your mind and intelligence fixed on Me, you will certainly come to Me.

A strategic vision will supply the organization with a set of objectives to be attained and a guiding purpose to direct itself through the changes brought by the environment. Leaders need to continually analyse the market changes and the competitive environment as well as the new opportunities in order they can act proactively side rather than a reactive side, which their teams might fall into.

A vision that is clearly communicated will be the basis of alignment throughout an organization, as the employees become more involved. When employees are aware of the company's mission and see the relationship with the work they do, they are more motivated and engaged. Leaders should regularly renew the vision through agendas like team meetings, goal setting conversations, and performance evaluations to be able to retain clarity and focus.

Avoiding Micromanagement

A leader who micromanages stifles creativity and reduces efficiency. They should put the tactical execution on the hand and let the team handle it, they themselves can focus on overseeing the strategic part. Set smart objectives and trust them to do their jobs, leaders are then better able to create a space where challenges are fun and where creativity is allowed to bloom.

Krishna advises against controlling every action:

"Prakrteh kriyamanani gunaih karmani sarvasah ahankara-vimudhatma kartaham iti manyate"

**प्रकृतैः क्रियमाणानि गुणैः कर्माणि सर्वशः।
आहंकारविमूढात्मा कर्ताहमिति मन्यते॥**

All activities are carried out by the three modes of material nature. But in ignorance, one who is deluded by the ego thinks himself to be the doer.

Leaders, when they micromanage, indirectly impair the members of the team to learn about problem-solving and trust in their own strength. Workers who are overly watched hesitate not only to take initiative, but also become disengaged, which in turn causes a workplace culture of dependency rather than innovation.

The correct relationship between the delegation and the trustee is that of trust. Managers must be specialists in the area of enabling employees to take control of their responsibilities and only intervene when guidance and help are requested. Stop over-specifying every aspect of the operation and focus on making an agreement with the employees for the goals to be met, ensuring that they figure out the best way for the tasks to be carried out.

Decision-Making in Complex Situations

Leadership is decision making and a continuous process. Leaders must balance data analytics with intuition and experience. However, the Bhagavad Gita tells us that one should act in a spirit of wisdom, being free from attachment and fear, for thinking about decisions. Mindfulness, as well as a strategic foresight, are necessary competencies for a leader to be able to cope with uncertainty.

Complex situations typically require a quick decision on the part of the leader, where the information may be fragmentary or even conflicting. At these times, leaders are not at liberty to make the choice solely based on logic. They must trust their intuition too. The data as well as insights are derived from analytics, but their use and understanding are still the domain of experience and prudence.

The mental aspect of mindfulness is the most important in decision-making. Leaders who work on self-awareness and emotional control will make logical choices, not irrational ones made under stress or impulsivity. They can make better choices aligned with long-term goals by their being present and examining situations from a distance.

Managing Resources Efficiently

Effective resource management is a critical aspect of implementing a balancing strategy. In addition to efficiently setting aside time, personnel, and financial resources, it is essential for leaders to ensure that these resources are allocated appropriately. This means that time, manpower, and money must be distributed effectively to achieve the desired outcomes.

Their successful resource management begins with the thorough understanding of the company's most important key areas. The leaders should make evaluations and decisions regarding what projects are able to meet company objectives and then they should prescribe the resources for each. This, in turn, is going to involve carefully planning and using data to make decisions which will make sure that the high-impact assignments will get the necessary support.

The development of time-saving strategies like task prioritization, delegation, and process automation will enable the leaders to enhance productivity as well as workflow optimization of the company. By engaging the team members in productive activities, there will be a decrease in the unnecessary effort and an increase in the general efficiency.

Conclusion

Leadership through Karma Sanyasa Yoga is an art of leading, by giving guidance, delegating, and empowering others, thus keeping the focus on higher objectives. A good method for leadership is time management. It is a form of empowerment in which the team is engrossed and motivated. The most important thing to consider is high-level strategy combined with tactical execution which needs vision, trust, and adaptability.

The final wisdom of the Gita reminds us:

"Sarva-dharmān parityajya mām ekaṃ śaraṇaṃ vraja ahaṃ tvāṃ sarva-pāpebhyo mokṣayiṣyāmi mā śucaḥ"

सर्वधर्मान् परित्यज्य मां एकं शरणं व्रज।
अहं त्वां सर्वपापेभ्यो मोक्षयिष्यामि मा शुचः॥

Abandon all varieties of dharma and just surrender unto Me. I shall deliver you from all sinful reactions. Do not fear.

With the coming together of such principles, leaders can create an atmosphere of cooperation, innovation, and top performance. The philosopher Krishna, in a similar fashion, heeded Arjuna's wisdom and clarity, which in the current times, leaders are needed to inspire confidence in their teams in the name of their teams' own performance. The main factor contributing to the success of the leadership is the ability to put the purpose, empower others, and make it clear that the execution strategies will change.

Leadership is not about controlling people; it is rather a process of helping them be a success. A leader that breeds the successful culture where trust is a standard, teams can learn through ongoing opportunities and the guide with the clear vision will succeed in the long-term based results. A truly effective leader understands that their role is not to micromanage but to provide direction and empowerment.

As leaders acknowledge the teachings of Karma Sannyasa Yoga, they are able to find the right way of dealing with their problems by working wise and gently, promising that both of their teams and themselves will be living in a world that is in a constant change. True leadership is a common goal, although the individual achievements are different from the Team's development. It is the legacy that they build that makes other people rise, contribute, and do something that leaves a lasting impression.

CHAPTER 5

Resilience And Perseverance (Dhyana Yoga)

An unavoidable part of the leadership journey is struggling with challenges, obstacles, and uncertainties; there is no way around them. If we decide to see emerging difficulties as our enemies, we will never grow the courage to withstand them, but if we determine to evaluate and face the challenges, we will develop the needed resiliency and perseverance for us to move ahead in our life. Through the ancient practice of Dhyana Yoga, the Bhagavad Gita expounds the virtues of inner strength, single-minded attention, and firm commitment to the goal are the path to success in our life.

A beautiful shloka from the Gita says:

"Yuktahara-viharasya yukta-cestasya karmasu yukta-svapnavabodhasya yogo bhavati duhkha-ha"

युक्ताहारविहारस्य युक्तचेष्टस्य कर्मसु।
युक्तस्वप्नावबोधस्य योगो भवति दुःखहा॥

One who is moderate in eating and recreation, balanced in work, and regulated in sleep and wakefulness, attains the yoga that destroys all suffering.

Resilience is the capacity to bounce back from setbacks, masterfully carry oneself during stress and come up with solutions when faced with problems. It is having integrity, not merely surviving until death. Leadership without integrity is autonomy.

To be exact, perseverance is the commitment to push on despite trials, failure, or setbacks. In fact, numerous grand personalities and institutions have undergone many fiascos before they achieved triumph. Focusing on performing tasks with dedication and being contentment with the long-term results contributes to success. Developing inner resilience at the top level of management helps them not only to persist but allows them to develop patience and perseverance as well.

Another way of developing leadership is through self-dedication and meditation on the path of Dhyana Yoga, the one also helps leaders to form an inner core that can withstand the stress of life, so they can always be resilient and perseverant in their goals. When a leader adopts mindful listening or deep reflection as part of their skillset, they are better equipped to make the right decisions, maintain a good inventory of their resources, and be more convinced even in complex situations.

The leaders who multiplied their success despite numerous challenges in the past are the most successful. These steadfast executives had a clear and unwavering vision and persevered in their mission to the end despite being hit by recession, interruptions of technology, or personal failures. The great leaders' exceptional quality comes from their ability to adapt, learn from their mistakes, and keep going persistently.

This section refers to how a designated person can strengthen their inner being, apply perseverance as a weapon, and maintain commitment to long-term objectives. An example of inclusion of such teachings would be another yoga teaching, Dhyana Yoga, through which individuals can develop mental and emotional resilience *"Success is impossible except a man meets his destiny bravely."*

The core of youth is not built through easy challenges but coping with those that they are not ready for. We can make great results when the art of reflection is combined with the effectiveness of a *"time bender"*. Leaders as problem-solvers certainly uplift themselves and others who are additionally motivated to persevere and accomplish.

Cultivating Inner Strength in Leadership

The Power of Inner Stability

Leadership is not just about outside achievements but about nurturing inner strength to endure adversities. The Bhagavad Gita has been asserting this for thousands of years. True strength is the ability to focus with an unwavering straight mind, and with this, one will be stable even in the midst of challenges. Leaders who become stable from inside reflect on the situation and then decide without being caught up in temporary defeats or emotional turmoil.

The Gita offers this wisdom:

"Prajahati yada kaman sarvan partha manogatan atmany evatmana tushtah sthita-prajnas tadocyate"

प्रजाहति यदा कामान् सर्वान् पार्थ मनोगतान्।
आत्मन्येवात्मना तुष्टः स्थितप्रज्ञस्तदोच्यते॥

When one gives up all desires of the mind, O Partha, and when his self is satisfied in the self, then he is said to be of steady wisdom.

Inner strength is the foundation of a leader who can remain calm under pressure, thereby ensuring that no stress or fear clouds their judgment. It is one of the factors that give way to concrete decision making and keep away from instant reaction, by choosing the right rational solutions. Leaders who are internally strong can evaluate solutions with realism and do critical risk analysis to come up with excellent strategies that not only their teams but also their organizations benefit from.

Moreover, inner stability leads to self-discipline, self-awareness, and sticking firmly to the end goals. In this reign, mental fitness exercises which are also a part of Dhyana Yoga, help the executives to maintain a certain level of mental sharpness and emotional toughness. When the brain is trained to focus on what is important, employees are left focused too and the boss can foresee the purpose the team needs to follow.

Furthermore, inner stability is the basis on which confidence and trust are built by a team. Employees look up to a leader who is not shaky and they feel comfortable besides being motivated to work harder. A calm and focused leader is the one who brings to bear the positive work environment that lights up the fire of resilience and perseverance in his employees.

Mindfulness and Focus

Meditation and mindfulness, which are activities that awaken the whole-brain, are tools that can provide a person with the essential knowledge required for spiritual evolution, progressive personal growth, and social perfection. It is a known fact that the strategic leaders must be perceptive of their inner selves and always make decisions based on the wisdom of the mind and not the impulse.

As Krishna advises in this beautiful shloka:

"Abhyasa-yoga-yuktena cetasa nanya-gamina paramam purusam divyam yati parthanucintayan"

अभ्यासयोगयुक्तेन चेतसा नान्यगामिना।
परमं पुरुषं दिव्यम् याती पार्थानुचिन्तयन्॥

By practicing yoga with a mind fixed on the Supreme Divine Person and not thinking of anything else, one attains the Supreme.

A leader who is more interested in their personal life needs to make self-reflection their habit even if it is not always practical. Best leaders have helped induce permanent ideology modification through reflection; they have the knowledge to abolish the status quo collectively and grow. After bringing in awareness, leaders can see the hurdles they face and, as a result, can perform better.

Teachers can build attention to a superpower when they show the characteristics of self-control, distress tolerance, and mindfulness too. On the other hand, students use a kind of meditation, e.g. walking. It is a belief that learners learn best when yoga is combined with lectures or be inserted into the curriculum in any other possible way.

Also, it helps them to see things positively which leads to a happier, healthier and more contented life. "To head it off at the pass" refers to overcoming obstacles. Besides, those who are able to be mindful are more adapted to being devoid of relationships and exerting effort in their acts.

Overcoming Fear and Doubt

According to Arjuna, fear and doubt can incapacitate decision-making. The teaching of Krishna to Arjuna in the Bhagavad Gita is to rise above his fears and make decisions. Thus, the leaders must be able to stifle self-doubt and be sure of the things they want. The art of developing resilience includes accepting the thoughts of fear but never acting according to them.

The Gita teaches us:

"Karmanye vadhikaraste ma phaleshu kadachana ma karma phala hetur bhurma te sangostva karmani"

कर्मण्येवाधिकारस्ते मा फलेषु कदाचन।
मा कर्मफलहेतुर्भूर्मा ते सङ्गोऽस्त्वकर्मणि॥

You have a right to perform your prescribed duty, but you are not entitled to the fruits of action. Never consider yourself the cause of the results of your activities, and never be attached to not doing your duty.

The eerie disquiet that comes with the fear of not being certified, of receiving crab on the prawn, or unpredictability is a situation that seems to have been tailored to leaders for not making a strong decision. Nonetheless, by having a mind frame that emanates trusting oneself and being courageous enough, the leaders will overcome the hesitation barrier and take the risks that they know they can handle. Probably, a wise leader will concede that fear is a natural emotion but to get over it should be a vital point.

Amidst the doubts one has to become mentally stronger, look for encouragement and be ready to learn from their errors. Leaders who use difficulties as opportunities for growth redeems the derivatives of the challenges in form of wisdom while learning. Transformation of the unknown place to the known makes problem-solving in the organization an easy task with active leaders being the first ones to act.

Through her example, the leader shows courage and becomes a source of encouragement for the team. When the followers learn of the leader conquering with confidence, they too adopt the no-fear lifestyle. This lauds the environment for not only innovation but also problem-solving and adaptability.

Emotional Intelligence in Leadership

A leader is considered strong and unwavering when they are emotionally intelligent. This includes the capacity to deal with stress, keep calm in case of difficult situations, and ability to establish a positive work atmosphere. When emotional regulation is the main focus of the leaders, team members have faith in them and a stable, trust-based atmosphere is created that is conducive to teamwork and the achievement of set goals.

Krishna teaches about this wisdom:

"Sukha-duhkhe same kritva labhalabhau jayajayau tato yuddhaya yujyasva naivam papam avapsyasi"

सुखदुःखेसमेकृत्वा लभालाभौ जयाजयौ।
ततो युद्धाय युज्यस्व नैवं पापमवाप्स्यसि॥

Being alike in pleasure and pain, gain and loss, victory and defeat, engage in the battle; thus, you shall not incur sin.

Emotional intelligence is the ability of leaders to handle different people by being aware of them and having compassion toward them. Mindfulness is practiced by being aware of one's own reactions felt, interpreting them and answering to challenges with patience and understanding. Emotional intelligence enables the leaders who grow up to communicate effectively, to be efficient during conflicts, and to keep the team morale high during tough days.

Emotional intelligent leaders foster a culture of mutual respect and collaboration. By practicing understanding and attentive listening, they create bonds with their team members and the team functions as a unit based on trust and solidarity. More so, emotional intelligence empowers leaders to be in control of their emotions and, as a result, remain calm and focused when in difficult situations.

Through the acquisition of the ability of emotional intelligence, the leaders, not only are the most effective in their own work, but also spread a positive attitude among their teams that leads to problems being approached with resilience, optimism, and unity. This emotional intelligence-based command nurtures a peaceful work environment and thus contributes to long-term business triumph.

Perseverance as a Strategic Advantage

The Role of Determination

A 'Never Give Up' attitude means the capability to stick to one's path regardless of the constraints that come along the way. Many of the biggest leaders and organizations were at some point or the other met with setbacks but they did not give up, they instead persevered, carried out their plans and finally succeeded. The Bhagavad Gita communicates that efforts must be persistent; then let go of the rewards and the success achieved in that situation will be the one that is the most fulfilling.

The Gita teaches the value of determination:

"Tasmat sarvesu kalesu mam anusmara yudhya ca mayy arpita-mano-buddhir mam evaisyasy asamsayah"

तस्मात्सर्वेषु कालेषु मां अनुस्मर युध्यच।
मय्यर्पितमनोबुद्धिरममेवैश्यस्यसंशयः॥

Therefore, remember Me at all times and fight. With your mind and intelligence fixed on Me, you will no doubt come to Me.

Determination is the force that moves leaders toward their goals even in the middle of a conflict and that is one of the key aspects of leadership. Only people who practice perseverance know that nothing is achieved overnight, and therefore have the ability to work consistently to be successful. To be loud and clear, it is the collective effort of a group of people who work hard, learn from their mistakes, and keep improving their strategies which leads to success. The challenge should be considered an opportunity to grow and quench the quest for consistently being the best.

Outstanding leaders are those who make good use of uncertainties and failures to thoroughly analyse all potential problems and come up with most effective solutions. They appreciate the problems that will come up as they pursue their purpose within different circumstances. These kinds of people have a specific code that enables them to stay in the act of leading their team even in the cheats when they set off on their mission with no view ahead.

Leaders, through perseverance, make their organizations prepare for the worst. Leadership is the art of showing by example and practicing the values of the entity when all odds are stacked against you. Whenever a squad witnesses this quality in the management, they get a positive attitude through appreciation to struggle as they will be seeing themselves the way leaders do. It is this capability to withstand, adjust, and continue that will bring about the success of both the team and the organization.

Learning from Setbacks

Failure is a stepping stone to improvement, and workers who learn to deal with setbacks as a part of learning and not a loss may find ways to improve their strategies and take better decisions. Krishna advises Arjuna to fight difficulties bravely, since without them we won't improve and make progress. He encourages him to be brave and learn from the battles.

As this powerful shloka states:

"Sthitva tasmin na dukhena gurunapi vicalyate tam vidyad duhkha-samyoga-viyogam yoga-samjnitam"

स्थित्वा तस्मिन्न दु:खेन गुरुनापि विचल्यते।
तम् विद्याद् दु:खसंयोगवियोगं योगसंज्ञितम्।।

Established in that state of yoga, one is not disturbed even by the greatest difficulties. This is known as the disconnection from the union with suffering.

The leader's resilience is measured in terms of their ability to draw usefully lessons from their failures. This is achieved by learning from the errors you have made and finding the necessary information to make the necessary changes in the future. This sort of thinking makes progress both in terms of creativity and improvement. A culture of learning makes an organization one of the best places to work, empowering employees to confidently face challenges and develop innovative, sometimes risky, solutions that help the company thrive.

In a situation when a firm fails, the leader's role is to use it as a basis for finding a solution rather than for blaming others. The constructive feedback approach can help organizations to build a creative and flexible team. This can be achieved by accepting shortcomings, discussing problems, and fine-tuning strategies through the insights gained from errors, which aid in preparing for the future.

Leaders who accept setbacks as a challenge from which they can learn something can turn trouble into opportunity. Each blow is a chance for the crew to re-frame goals, outline strategies which are more effective and skilfully develop the ability to cope with the problems that arise. Therefore, by being emotionally flexible and by being prepared to compromise, leaders can consolidate their position as well as the companies they run for the long hall of prosperity.

Building a Resilient Organization

An organization that is resilient is one that can change without losing its main purpose. The leaders of the organization have to be able to create a culture where resilience is admired, where the failures are looked at as an instrument of learning, and the ability is exercised by the workers to go ahead no matter what the barrier is.

The Gita provides this wisdom:

"Yogasthah kuru karmani sangam tyaktva dhananjaya siddhyasiddhyoh samo bhutva samatvam yoga ucyate"

योगस्थो कुरु कर्माणि सङ्गं त्यक्त्वा धनञ्जय।
सिद्ध्यसिद्ध्योः समो भूत्वा समत्वं योग उच्यते॥

Perform your duty equally poised in success and failure. Such equanimity is called yoga.

Resilient organizations highlight flexibility, innovation, and problem-solving. By putting in place the systems that promote adaptability, the leaders can be sure that their teams will be flexible even in the case of industry changes. This entails the creation of a workplace that not only values persistence but also supports employees to become more creative and take initiative to overcome obstacles.

To promote corporate creativity, organizations are required to invest in employee development which in turn will ensure that every staff member is competent and self-assured to cope with ambiguity. The promotion of a proactive mindset through which employees can foresee and prepare for difficulties enhances the endurance of the entire organization.

Open dialogue and transparency are also very important. The line managers need to set clear goals, give constant feedback, and unveil a safe atmosphere for the workers to voice their concerns and propose their ideas. When the teams are well-supported, they can easily adapt and also find innovative solutions to their problems.

Staying Committed to Long-Term Strategic Goals

Vision-Driven Leadership

Leader possessing a well-articulated vision is more likely to perceive the value of taking the hard way to meet the long-term goals. The Bhagavad Gita claims that targeted activities are better than purposeless activities. Managers must declare their objectives clearly and make sure that each step that they take corresponds with the framework of their bigger objective.

The Gita offers this insight:

"Tapasvibhyo 'dhiko yogi jnanibhyo 'pi mato 'dhikah karmibhyas cadhiko yogi tasmad yogi bhavarjuna"

तपस्विभ्यो 'धिको योगी ज्ञानिभ्यो 'पि मतो 'धिकः।
कर्मिभ्यश्चाधिको योगी तस्माद्योगी भव अर्जुन॥

A yogi is greater than the ascetic, greater than the empiricist, and greater than the fruitive worker. Therefore, be a yogi, O Arjuna.

A vision that is both compelling and challenging inspires a strong sense of purpose and unites teams around a common goal. Visionary leaders who communicate their dreams with passion engage employees, helping them feel like integral parts of that vision and fostering deep commitment. When employees understand how their individual contributions drive the team's overall success, they participate more actively and demonstrate greater enthusiasm for achieving the desired outcomes.

Besides, a strong vision enables leaders to be at ease while steering through uncertain conditions. In moments of crisis, a well-declared purpose is the star that shows the strategic path directing that the decisions be made in favour of long-term goals. By continuously reminding staff of the bigger vision, leaders are able to instil sustainability, resourcefulness, and resilience to remain focused and motivated despite the challenging times.

Vision-based management, with its emphasis on the development of a society that is based on resolute intentions, flexibility, and the welfare of others is a sure way to ensure success together with your team.

Inspiring Others to Stay Committed

A leader's sacrificing spirit influences the whole team profoundly. Resilience being the leader's virtue, he or she uplifts the team not only to be dedicated, but to be motivated and to focus on the long-term goals. The leader's determination in the face of adversity inspires them to work with the same level of commitment and dedication.

Krishna reminds us:

"Yadyad acarati sresthas tat tad evetaro janah sa yat pramanam kurute lokas tad anuvartate"

यद्यदाचरति श्रेष्ठस्तत्तदेवेतरो जनः।
स यत्प्रमाणं कुरुते लोकस्तदअनुवर्तते॥

Whatever a great person does, common men follow. Whatever standards he sets by exemplary acts, all the world pursues.

Leaders who maintain a strong passion for their vision lay the foundation for confidence—the essential ingredient of trust, loyalty, and a shared sense of purpose within the team. When employees understand the significance of their roles and feel genuinely appreciated, they become more engaged and motivated to go the extra mile to achieve the common goal.

To make their staff determined, the leaders need to be precise in amassing the team and provide the necessary guidance to them in times that are challenging. This establishes the workplace as the constructive environment, where the staff believes that problems are just an attempt at improvement rather than the stopping force.

Leaders can build resilience in their teams and emphasize sustainability and durability of team commitment through their confidence by which they set plain long-term goals and assure the team of the same.

Staying Motivated Through Challenges

The motivation levels of one can be up and down, but the discipline is what helps to keep them committed to their goals. Leaders themselves and their teams need to have an established routine or system in place, where both, a and b simultaneously are motivated. One way to reach the final objective is by dividing it into small tasks, which are easy to achieve and help one move towards the accomplishing of bigger goals.

The wisdom of the Gita guides us:

"Niyatam kuru karma tvam karma jyayo hy akarmanah sarira-yatrapi ca te na prasiddhyed akarmanah"

नियतं कुरु कर्म त्वं कर्म ज्यायो ह्यकर्मणः।
शरीरयात्रापि च ते न प्रसिद्ध्येदकर्मणः।।

Perform your prescribed duty, for doing so is better than not working. One cannot even maintain one's physical body without work.

Motivation resulting from within (intrinsic motivation), when driven by the purpose of living beings and when flowing from the passion of one's unique life purpose prolongs patient endings. Those leaders who can clarify their goals and tie them to those worthy goals are more capable of creating an environment conducive to fun and engaged workers.

Moreover, it would appear that one of the skills effective leaders shall have is the ability to promote a climate of support and motivation. The company may choose to improve the engagement by recognizing the contributions of employees and allowing them to acquire new skills. Once employees start to comprehend their own value and engage with the termination objectives of the firm, a connection and commitment will be fostered.

By management of motivation through discipline, involvement of a clear vision, and steady reinforcement, leaders can maintain the energy and focusing of their teams, ensuring long-term benefits even in the tough times.

Conclusion

Resilience and perseverance are the key characteristics which define the leaders who stand in the face of challenges, setbacks, and uncertainties. In addition, leaders must also grow their mental and emotional strength to get through the difficulties. The Bhagavad Gita is one of the thunderous books which proves that the true success of those is who have unshakeable faith in what they are doing even when they fail temporarily or the outside forces.

The final shloka of this chapter reminds us:

"Om tat sat iti nirdeso brahmanas tri-vidhah smrtah brahmanas tena vedas ca yajnas ca vihitah pura"

ॐ तत्सत् इति निर्देशो ब्राह्मणस्त्रिविधः स्मृतः।
ब्राह्मणस्तेन वेदाश्च यज्ञाश्च विहितः पुरा॥

Om, tat, and sat. This threefold designation of the Supreme is remembered by the knowers of Brahman. By this were the brahmanas, the Vedas, and sacrifices ordained of old.

Perseverance does not only mean that one is persistent but also that one has the inner clarity, focus, and dedication in the light of adversity. A leader who is able to keep the spirit of determination alive in their personnel can encourage the culture of dedication and innovation. Through setting up environments where setbacks are considered as learning experiences, they help people be inspired to take initiatives and remain motivated.

It is a proven fact that true resilience is not just about protection but it is about the process of becoming a better person. An organization whose leaders are trained in these areas can be resilient even in the midst of volatile periods. By means of resilience and perseverance, they not only reach their own goals but also make a significant contribution in the benefit of future generations.

CHAPTER 6

Ethical Conduct (Sthitaprajna Lakshana Yoga)

One of the most crucial elements of ethical leadership and strategy is that ethics is not merely a trait of a good leader—it forms the very foundation of sustainable success. The Bhagavad Gita teaches about the concept of **Sthitaprajna** - a person who is self-aware and enlightened, embodying unwavering wisdom and righteousness. Such a leader remains steady and unswayed by external pressures. For any company or organization to achieve true success, ethical decision-making must be at its core. This requires leaders who command respect and loyalty, supported by an organizational culture grounded in clear, steadfast values that guide every action.

The Gita describes the Sthitaprajna in this beautiful shloka:

"Prajahati yada kaman sarvan partha manogatan atmany evatmana tushtah sthitaprajnas tadocyate"

प्रजाहति यदा कामान् सर्वान् पार्थ मनोगतान्।

आत्मन्येवात्मना तुष्टः स्थितप्रज्ञस्तदोच्यते॥

When a person abandons all desires that arise in the mind, O Partha, and remains satisfied in the self by the self, then he is called a person of steady wisdom.

The present-day corporate world is gummed up with complex ethical quandaries. The questions that now arise are - how a leader can choose to adhere to ethical practices over financial gains in their organization. Nevertheless, true leadership means one that will have to sacrifice their desires for the common good. The Bhagavad Gita preaches that the right activity done with knowledge and without the pursuit of personal gains is the cause of the prosperity that stays. Ethical leadership is more than just following the rules and regulations, it's about creating such a work environment that moral and ethical issues will be deeply embedded.

Those companies that are driven by honesty and ethics in their strategic framework, are bound to give birth to a culture of truth and reliability. Workers are more motivated and productive in an environment where they are not asked to compromise on their principles, and clients are more willing to invest in businesses that are equipped with a strong ethical framework. Apart from business gains, unethical activities have more or less far-reaching damage that may involve legal bonds, and reputation loss.

This chapter elucidates three pivotal aspects of moral aptitude in leadership and strategy. Initially, we scrutinize the implementation of ethics into strategic decision-making, making it certain that enterprises make the right choice of not only acquiring profit but also keeping their stakeholders and society in mind. Secondly, we talk about the significance of integrity in leadership by specifying how those leaders who live by ethical values can gain trust and attain prosperity that is long-term. Lastly, we delve into the concept of strategic alignment that companies can apply when ethics are at the core of the decision a company makes, which can result in the emergence of exceptional corporate cultures that not only represent ethical conduct but rather are intrinsically embedded in each facet of the company.

Integrating Ethics into Strategic Decisions

The Importance of Ethical Decision-Making

As the economy accelerates, CEOs may face situations where financial gains appear to conflict with ethical principles. However, the Bhagavad Gita teaches that true success arises from aligning with the universe's moral harmony—making decisions guided by profound wisdom and an understanding beyond the ego's selfish desires, rather than being driven by short-term gains.

As Krishna advises in this powerful shloka:

"Karmanye vadhikaraste ma phaleshu kadachana ma karma phala hetur bhurma te sangostva karmani"

कर्मण्येवाधिकारस्ते मा फलेषु कदाचन।
मा कर्मफलहेतुर्भूर्मा ते सङ्गोऽस्त्वकर्मणि।।

You have the right to perform your prescribed duties, but you are not entitled to the fruits of your actions. Never consider yourself to be the cause of the results of your activities, and never be attached to not doing your duty.

Ethical decision-making processes include the following:

1. **Assessing Consequences:** While leaders who demonstrate the principles of ethical leadership and

ethical leadership consider 'both' long and short-term employment effects on all these groups in the process of consequences, they are supposed to make decisions based on considered results.

2. **Fairness and Transparency In decision-making:** Fairness and Transparency are important because they're considering all parties, such as workers, clients, and society. The organization should preserve that element and not choose financial profit only. Ethical leaders not only communicate openly but also provide equal opportunities and make the right choice by ensuring trust and making decisions without any prejudices.
3. **Clarity of Purpose:** An organization is said to have clarity of purpose when each choice made is in line with the fundamental values and long-term goals of the organization. When leaders don't desert their mission, they bring into being the constancy, inspire trust, and propagate a tough ethical culture. A crystal-clear vision facilitates the organizations in dealing with problems without losing the moral values and strategic objectives they have set their eyes on.
4. **Courage to Do the Right Thing:** The willingness to do the right thing is not to be understood as standing in the way of ethical values even if faced by pressure, opposition, and short-term losses. The genuine leaders will resist the temptation of using shortcuts, as well as strictly keeping the integrity issue for the sake of quick gains.

Real-World Applications of Ethical Strategies

In recent years, some of the world's most prominent commercial enterprises have enhanced their market presence by demonstrating that ethical business practices and profitability can go hand in hand. Companies such as Tata Group, Patagonia, and Unilever have integrated ethical principles into their core strategies, proving that organizations grounded in integrity can not only achieve sustainable growth but also create a positive impact on society.

The Gita offers this wisdom for ethical action:

"Yad yad acarati sresthas tat tad evetaro janah sa yat pramanam kurute lokas tad anuvartate"

यद्यदाचरति श्रेष्ठस्तत्तदेवेतरो जनः।
स यत्प्रमाणं कुरुते लोकस्तदअनुवर्तते॥

Whatever action is performed by a great person, others follow in his footsteps. Whatever standards he sets, the world pursues.

Take the Tata Group as an example, they have built a good public image due to their ethical business practices where employees get fair treatment and the firm participates in socially responsible actions. Their first and foremost concern has been for integrity and community welfare. Hence, Tata Group is one of the most respected business conglomerates. In a similar vein, Patagonia has established a gold standard with the other major American outdoor gear companies for the sustainability of environmental resources. Through the use of eco-friendly production, responsible sourcing, and fair labour practices, these customers have become more loyal and it is this particular aspect that has proven that ethical businesses can also be highly profitable but only when sustainability is also a part of corporate strategy.

For businesses that prioritize ethics as the foundation of their decision-making process, they are helping to establish a trust culture that extends to everybody including employees, customers, and investors. Through this, employees feel secure as they are treated fairly, customers are loyal to brands they trust and the investors know they are stable and have a long-term potential of success when they do their business ethically.

The Role of Integrity in Leadership

Integrity as the Foundation of Strong Leadership

The need for leaders with integrity cannot be overstressed. Honesty and respect to people is the true sign of the right character. To read on, our analogy will help you to see it in a significant way. Integrity is the foundation of the real development and gives the necessary support to credibility to overcome the problems arising with the flow. In Bhagavad Gita, it is specified that a leader is one who is not only well-acquainted with the work requirements but is also honest, firm, and committed to the right causes.

The Gita illuminates this wisdom:

"Anudvega-karam vakyam satyam priya-hitam ca yat svadhyayabhyasanam caiva van-mayam tapa ucyate"

अनुद्वेगकरं वाक्यम् सत्यं प्रियहितं च यत्।
स्वाध्यायाभ्यासनं चैव वन्मयं तप उच्यते॥

Speech that causes no distress, that is truthful, pleasant and beneficial and the regular recitation of sacred texts; these constitute the austerity of speech.

Leaders who uphold integrity and earn the trust of their teams foster loyalty and build a culture of accountability, striving consistently to deliver on their promises. By setting an example of transparency as well as ethical principles, they develop organizations that are resilient, respected, and successful in the long run.

A leader with integrity:

1. **Leads by Example:** True leaders don't just express their expectations; they embody them in their daily interactions with others. They follow through on what they ask of others, demonstrating that honesty, decency, and respect are the values they uphold.
2. **Builds Trust:** The foundation of effective leadership is to instil trust in people. The ones who use ethical means are the only leaders who can earn the trust of their followers through being consistently open, fair, and transparent. When leaders show their integrity, and are open and honest to their employees in their decisions, employees feel safe and valued, and thus are motivated to strive to achieve goals.
3. **Takes Responsibility:** The leader who takes the blame– the real one, does not hand it to another person or simply shun the task. Instead, they confess the error, assumes the blame for the behaviour, and dwells on gaining new knowledge and experience. That ego check and corporate culture make it easier for everyone to be honest and for the business to be in a state of constant reformation.
4. **Puts Long-Term Vision Over Short-Term Gains:** Ethical leadership has been raising the bar when it comes to corporate decision-making, whereby sustainable profitability is prized much more than instantaneous wins. It means that their

decisions make sure their base is sound and that they are creating not just today but also in the future the required value that really brings happiness to people.

Why Integrity Matters in Leadership

Leaders who have integrity will still stick with their principles in the face of any external pressures, tough choices or opposition. Throughout the Bhagavad Gita, Arjuna was advised by Krishna to act with the awareness of righteousness, just as the ethical leaders need to rely on their inner moral compass to get them on the right path during difficult times.

The Gita guides us with this wisdom:

"Sukha-duhkhe same kritva labhalabhau jayajayau tato yuddhaya yujyasva naivam papam avapsyasi"

सुखदु:खेसमेकृत्वा लभालाभौ जयाजयौ।
ततो युद्धाय युज्यस्व नैवं पापमवाप्स्यसि॥

Having made pleasure and pain, gain and loss, victory and defeat the same, engage in battle for the sake of battle; thus, you will incur no sin.

A commitment to personal integrity paves the way for building organizational cultures rooted in justice and ethical treatment. Ethical leaders transform the world by empowering people to embrace the principle that "doing the right thing" is always rewarded and valued.

Integrity in leadership is thought of as a trust climate and an attribute of self-accountability. The long-term trust of the teams, customers, and stakeholders is the price that they get when leaders act in an ethical and honest manner continually. Increasingly, employees are at peace knowing that their leaders will act with justice, customers getting loyalty from the brands that implement integrity and investors giving weight to the organizations that hold up long-term ethical norms.

Case Study: Satya Nadella's Ethical Leadership

While Satya Nadella was at the helm of Microsoft, one of the very first steps he took was to bring about a change in the culture of the organization by promoting a culture of empathy, inclusion, and ethical leadership in its core operations. Knowing that a toxic work environment is the root cause of lack of innovation, he modelled and encouraged a growth mindset by allowing employees to engage in introspection and mission.

Krishna's guidance in the Gita parallels this approach:

"Atmany eva ca santustah tasya karyam na vidyate na casya sarva-bhutesu kascid artha-vyapasrayah"

आत्मन्येव च संतुष्टः तस्य कार्यं न विद्यते।
न चास्य सर्वभूतेषु कश्चिदर्थव्यापाश्रयः॥

For one who is content within himself and finds satisfaction within the self, there is no duty nor any need to perform any action.

It further went to the extent of introducing chemicals, which are environment-friendly as well as made out of recycling to the consumers. On the other side, he has put a great emphasis on the driver's ego-destroying development system giving the impression that the car is superfluous. Nevertheless, the ethical AI approach concentrates on unbiased and responsible AI technology application. By demonstrating a people-first and ethical approach, he underscores the importance of people-focused decision-making and creating a positive work environment that is key to both business success and company longevity.

Aligning Organizational Strategy with Ethical Principles

Building an Ethical Work Culture

To be a truly ethical organization that effectively serves its purposes and achieves its targets, genuine ethics must be practiced consistently. An organization's ethics should go beyond simply defining its mission; they must be embedded in the company's policy framework, hiring processes, the behavior of top management, and all organizational initiatives.

The Gita teaches this wisdom about ethical conduct:

"Ahimsa satyam akrodhas tyagah santir apaisunam daya bhutesv aloluptvam mardavam hrir acapalam"

अहिंसा सत्यं अक्रोधस्त्यागः शान्तिरअपैसुंनं।
दया भूतेष्वलोलुप्त्वं मार्दवं ह्रीरचापलम्॥

Non-violence, truthfulness, freedom from anger, renunciation, tranquillity, aversion to fault-finding, compassion for all beings, freedom from covetousness, gentleness, modesty, and absence of fickleness.

1. **Creating Clear Ethical Guidelines:** A company must have very clear rules about right and wrong. If everyone knows the rules, they can all follow them. This makes the company better. The company rules cover interests of conflicts, dealing with others, how employees behave, and company duties to society. Being aware of

the rules gives workers confidence and shows everyone the company is just and reliable.

2. **Training and Development: Training** and development program are important in order to integrate ethical practices into the company. By teaching ethics in a structured way, the company ensures that the employees have the knowledge and skills required to identify complex moral dilemmas and to know how to act in the workplace. Ethical education is a continuous process that would bring about employees who see the importance of being fair, accountable, and making smart decisions
3. **Encouraging Open Communication:** For a strong ethical workplace culture, open lines of communication need to be fostered. Such that employees should be able to report unethical behaviour without being afraid of being treated with retaliation or in a negative manner.
4. **Recognizing and Rewarding Ethical Behaviour:** Companies can encourage ethical behaviour by acknowledging and rewarding ethical conduct. This creates a positive reinforcement mechanism that promotes both individual and team-based ethical decisions. Recognition can come in many forms, from formal awards and bonuses to simple acknowledgments in team meetings.

Ethical Strategy in Business Operations

Strategic planning that corresponds to ethical principles is an essential requirement for organizations aiming to acquire strong, long-term success, and thoroughly combat ability. This is mostly due to the fact that they achieve the confidence of their staff, customers, shareholders, and other critical stakeholders by giving priority to elements such as justice, transparency, and corporate social responsibility.

Krishna provides this guidance:

"Sarva-bhuteshu yenaikam bhavam avyayam ikshate avibhaktam vibhakteshu taj jnanam viddhi sattvikam"

सर्वभूतेषु येनैकं भावमव्ययम् इच्छते।
अविभक्तं विभक्तेषु तज्ज्ञानं विद्धि सात्त्विकम्॥

That knowledge by which one undivided spiritual nature is seen in all existences, undivided in the divided is knowledge in the mode of goodness.

1. **Fair Labour Practices:** An ethical working environment is the foremost ingredient for the production of a socially responsible and profitable enterprise. This should be manifested by the offering of reasonable salaries, the provision of secure and healthy workplace conditions, and the promotion of the overall well-being of the employees.
2. **Sustainability Initiatives:** Sustainability programs are very important in decreasing a company's footstep on the world and in maintaining equilibrium in nature for a long period. Eco-friendly methods in the form of waste reduction, carbon emission decrease, and the production of renewable energy are all part of the environmental destruction solution.
3. **Honest Marketing and Customer Relations:** Consequently, strong customer relations are needed and transparency is essential for marketing and brand loyalty. Companies should avoid misleading

advertisements, exaggerated claims, or deceptive pricing tactics, as these can damage credibility and customer satisfaction.

4. **Social Responsibility:** In the eyes of the sustainable development of responsible business, social responsibility is the key. Through this, importance is given to the company's giving and participation in the community for societal praises Organizations benefit, philanthropic causes are promoted, environmental sustainability is employed, and sustainable development is practiced by them.

Conclusion

The foundation of a community's success in leadership and management lies in ethical conduct. The Bhagavad Gita conveys the message of a steadfast leader who follows a divine path, remaining unwavering despite external pressures. In today's fast-paced and competitive world, upholding these principles is especially challenging. Ethical leadership, therefore, is not merely a matter of conscience—it is a strategic necessity.

The final wisdom of this chapter from the Gita:

"Samatvam yoga ucyate yogah karmasu kausalam"

समत्वं योग उच्यते योगः कर्मसु कौशलम्॥

Equanimity is called yoga; yoga is skilfulness in action.

By embracing a strong set of ethical values, organizational leadership transcends mere compliance with laws and regulations. This commitment reflects a willingness to make the right choices, even when they are difficult or subtle. A leader guided by integrity exemplifies accountability, complete transparency, and fairness. As a result, the organization benefits from more engaged employees, stronger customer relationships, and greater resilience in the face of challenges.

By adopting the Sthitaprajna Lakshana Yoga methods the leaders may deal with the complexity of the business environment confidently and wisely. Thus, ethical decision-making becomes the leading principle that assures harm to the longevity of the organization and a good name. Finally, true prosperity is not counted among mere financial profits but according to the unfading effect of an organization on society this and future generation will have. By putting ethics first, leaders and organizations can set up an atmosphere of community where people can rely on, be responsible for actions, and achieve meaningful outcomes through the best use of the resources of the community.

CHAPTER 7

Mindfulness and Focus (Dhyana Yoga)

In this fast-paced world we are constantly surrounded by distractions. Leaders and strategists have to multitask and also be torn in different directions at the same time, which makes it difficult for them to focus on what is important.

To be able to make the kind of strategic choices that are pragmatic requires a clear head, the ability to concentrate and presence of mind. The teachings of the Bhagavad Gita would suggest the use of meditation as a way to attain it and be able to develop mindfulness and focus. In this way, they are able to assess the situation as problematic, not as threatening and hence make the more optimal and thoughtful decision through this pacing practice.

A profound shloka in the Gita tells us:

"yuktahara-viharasya yukta-cestasya karmasu yukta-svapnavabodhasya yogo bhavati duhkha-ha"

युक्ताहारविहारस्य युक्तचेष्टस्य कर्मसु।
युक्तस्वप्नावबोधस्य योगो भवति दुःखहा।।

For one who is moderate in eating and recreation, balanced in work, and regulated in sleep and wakefulness, yoga becomes the destroyer of suffering.

Mindfulness goes far beyond meditation; it is being truly present and fully involved in the moment, making conscious choices, and managing resources with effectiveness and efficiency. Mindful leaders are able to see through the noise and can keep their sight on their goals without being distracted thus can maintain a culture of solid and conscious decision making. As the leader goes deep into a task, there is a manifest increase in productivity, the ability to solve problems, and make better progress towards a goal.

In the business realm, leaders face challenges such as strict time constraints, numerous conflicting priorities, and the need to balance long-term planning with short-term actions. When decision-making is compromised by external pressures and sudden impulses, it often leads to impaired outcomes. But, happiness and the achievement of goals are possible only when these actions have the power that comes from being based on a clear sense of purpose i.e. persistence and productivity that bring success.

Leaders can acquire a clear, patient, and successful approach in both their personal and professional spheres by these methods.

Strategic Decision-Making with Mindfulness

The Power of Mindfulness in Leadership

Mindfulness refers to the capability of staying present and being fully engaged in the current moment reflecting the Bhagavad Gita, which is a leadership strategy. It allows a leader to recognize situations, think effectively, and take good decisions based on composure in psychological functions. Arjuna's enlightening knowledge and Krishna's wise counselling still reach out to the readers of the Bhagavad Gita. In the midst of a battle on the battlefield, the mind of the warrior will walk away, make bad decisions and come back without any ideas. Likewise, the present-day leaders, who have mastered the tool of mindfulness, are able to understand their path with clarity and confidence.

The Gita teaches us:

"dhyayato visayan pumsah sangas tesupajayate
sangat sanjayate kamah kamat krodho 'bhijayate"

ध्यानतो विषयान्पुम्सः सङ्गस्तेषुपजायते।
सङ्गात्सञ्जायते कामः कामात्क्रोधो 'भिजायते॥

When a person dwells on the objects of the senses, attachment to them develops. From attachment arises desire, and from desire arises anger.

When the mindfulness in decision-making drives leaders, they become immune to hasty, emotional decisions and end up making better decisions. What the leaders do instead is study their environment, making sure that the short-term as well as the protracted effect are equally taken into account. This is the way it leads to a lower level of risk, a better way to deal with problems and a more ethical way of dealing with decisions.

A mindful leader examines every decision with full awareness, besides looking at the financial outcomes of the issue, ethical considerations, and the alignment of the solution with the broader strategic intent. Through the skill of being in the moment and not being caught up in distractions the leaders will be able to see the whole picture of a situation and make decisions that will be in line with their vision and values.

Practical Techniques for Mindful Decision-Making

1. **Pause Before Reacting:** Before you make a crucial choice, take time to breathe and calm down. This way emotional reactions are out of the picture and instead rational thinking is stimulated. When leaders have to confront stressful situations, they frequently feel an urge to respond immediately. But by taking a short time to wait, one can adopt a calmer, deeper and purer approach. A few seconds of inward-looking prompts leaders to evaluate the state of affairs impartially and by means of that process, they are able to examine different views thus see lasting results. This uncomplicated ritual is the best strategy for preventing hasty decisions that can trigger off negative consequences.

As the Gita reminds us:

"indriyani parany ahur indriyebhyah param manah manasas tu para buddhir yo buddheh paratas tu sah"

इन्द्रियाणि पराण्याहुरिन्द्रियेभ्य: परं मन:।
मनसस्तु परा बुद्धिर्यो बुद्धे: परतस्तु स:॥

The senses are superior to the body, the mind is superior to the senses, the intelligence is superior to the mind, and the soul is superior to the intelligence.

2. **Active Listening:** Team members, customers, and stakeholders should be listened to without being interrupted or pushed to conclusions by leaders. The majority of leaders are trapped in the cycle of hearing

only what they want to hear or preparing a response. When it comes to active listening, we are talking about the ability to pay complete attention, wait for the right moment to speak, and be open-minded. Everyone must pay attention to the words, tone, and body language that they employ when communicating with others and be cautious about jumping to a conclusion. Demonstrating the skill of being active listener leaders are able to develop better relationships, make better decisions, and establish a respectful and trusting environment in their teams.

3. **Single-Tasking Over Multitasking:** One problem should get the attention of dialogue. Even though the process of multitasking may seem efficient, it usually results in mistakes and ultimately lower productivity creating fatigue of the brain. Therefore, one problem should get the attention of dialogue. All tasks that are able to fully capture the attention of the leader are likely to produce a clear understanding and higher level of retention of the final product.
4. **Journaling and Reflection:** Putting down thoughts and dissecting decisions can undoubtedly provide clear markers of a storyline and help to see the patterns over a period of time. Keeping a journal is a strategy for leaders, where they can observe their thoughts, accept challenges they may face, and revise their past decisions. This procedure enhances their mind-to-self detection and correction capability to understand the affectations and biases that encumber their creative thinking, thus enabling them to improve. A deeper reflection will allow the individual to maximize the learning process and develop self-awareness, which will increase the accuracy

of decision-making and the ability to solve problems effectively and creatively.

5. **Guided Visualization:** To visualize seriously, look into the future of different ideas in your head seems to be valuable in the decision-making process. A leader can identify potential problems, interpret possible threats, and select the best way to act by creating a mental picture of the most likely situations. Implementing this method allows one to acquire the ability to foresee the future, become a more efficient decision-maker, and shape leaders for the ever-changing reality, as they mentally get the practice of their tactics before the actual post.

Focused Attention and Resource Allocation

Why Focus Matters in Strategy?

An unorganized mind leads to disjointed work. The capability of executives and managers to concentrate on the most critical areas is the key determinant factor of success in business and leadership. The focal attention guarantees that resources no matter what they are, time, money, or human capital, are put to use in the right way.

The Gita offers this insight:

"ekagram manah kritva yat jnana-vijnana-trptah kutasthah vijita-atma yogayukta-atma sarvatra sama-darsanah"

एकाग्रमण: कृत्वा यत्ज्ञानविज्ञानतृप्त:।

कूटस्थ: विजितात्मा योगयुक्तात्मा सर्वत्र समदर्शना।।

With a single-pointed mind, satiated with knowledge and realization, unwavering and with conquered senses, the yogi sees the same everywhere.

Krishna counsels Arjuna to concentrate on his own task, without being frightened or lured by desires. This principle also works in leadership: the greatest energy of the company is concentrated on the mission and vision which causes distractions to be less likely and hence the projects to continue the way they are supposed to.

Lack of focus can lead to wasted resources, poor execution, and missed opportunities. Companies that maintain transparency in their strategic goals are better equipped to channel their energy towards meaningful initiatives that drive long-term growth. Leaders should encourage their teams to eliminate distractions and concentrate on activities aligned with the organization's objectives.

Allocating Resources Wisely

The practice of strategic management wisdom states that not all projects are equal or, in a start-up, they won't all be eligible for the maximum investment. It is a means of gaining full competition in the various dimensions (*strategic, operational, and financial*). Although the road is not easy, people must persist in doing so.

Krishna advises:

"yatah pravrttir bhutanam yena sarvam idam tatam sva-karmana tam abhyarcya siddhim vindati manavah"

यतः प्रवर्तिरभूतानां येन सर्वमिदं ततं।

स्वकर्मणा तमभ्यर्च्य सिद्धिमिन्दति मानवः॥

By worshiping through one's own duties the source from whom all beings arise and by whom all this is pervaded, a person attains perfection.

1. **Identify High-Impact Areas:** Not all projects matter the same to a business. Leaders should find and fund crucial efforts that bring the most worth. This involves studying what the company wants, what clients need, and what's going on in the market. By focusing on things that fit with long-term goals, businesses can do things smarter and make sustainable progress. Prioritizing high-value projects keeps resources from wasting money, staff time, and energy making companies more competitive.
2. **Set Clear Goals:** In order to stop the waste of efforts, the success of each campaign should be pointed out. The goals let employees know where to move and are the first conditions that make strategic priorities fulfilled among the organizations. Are the leg transfers getting underway when the leaders write out the methods that are going to be employed? Therefore, they ensure proper usage of the resources and progress is well monitored.
3. **Delegate Effectively:** Entrust employees with tasks that correspond to their strong skills and thus, create time, for decision-making of higher level. Delegation makes it possible for leaders to keep their attention on the most important goals while also encouraging team members to become owners of their tasks. When tasks are distributed according to each person's area of expertise, both productivity and organizational efficiency grow.

4. **Use Data-Driven Insights:** Employ data mining techniques to analyze past performance indicators and current market trends before planning resource allocation. Leaders can leverage this data to make informed decisions, identify challenges, and develop solutions grounded in evidence rather than speculation. This approach ensures that investments are directed towards high-impact areas, thereby maximizing ROI and promoting sustainable business operations.
5. **Avoid Overcommitment:** Overburdening yourself with tasks could make you lose that focus and eventually, have you end up quitting the job. Instead, set out the few broadly defined strategic objectives that you wish to make sure your teams enable to happen. Leaders normally manage to work productively without burning out when they avoid the temptation to do too much. Organizations become more proficient in their work, reduce pressure, and develop a culture of strategic discipline by emphasizing only the key tasks.

Enhancing Concentration for Effective Strategy Execution

The Role of Concentration in Execution

Simply having a well-thought-out strategy is not enough, as only proper execution leads to success. For accomplishing our plans, concentration is a vital characteristic. It's possible that the lack of it brings in the distraction and inefficiencies that eventually result in delays and below-par performances.

The Gita teaches:

"yato yato niscarati manas cancalam asthiram
tatas tato niyamyaitad atmany eva vasam nayet"

यतो यतो निश्चरति मनश्चञ्चलमस्थिरम्।
ततस्ततो नियम्यैतदात्मन्येव वशं नयेत्॥

Wherever the mind wanders, restless and unsteady, one should bring it back, controlled, to the self.

In the Bhagavad Gita, Krishna emphasizes on Ekagrata: concentration of the single point. Leaders who gain a strong focus on a particular thing are the ones who can get by challenges effortlessly and exhibit skills in the fields they choose. A centred mind with sustained effort ensures that leaders are capable of reaching their goals with the help of creativity and versatility. A correct approach is also reinforced through this, as leaders are able to concentrate on their objectives without falling into a trap of switching to other tasks too often. This results in confidence that their strategies will not only be well-planned but also executed efficiently.

Techniques to Improve Concentration

1. **Eliminate Distractions:** There are a lot of things going on that make it hard for someone to work. People need periods of time where they can concentrate without interruptions from other people. This might include a number of techniques including getting rid of sounds from other technologies, making a schedule that includes periods of time to concentrate on an assigned task. Bringing order to one's space can also help to increase the ability to concentrate. Doing only one thing at a time can help people concentrate more deeply while at work.

Krishna advises:

"abhyasena tu kaunteya vairagyena ca grhyate"

अभ्यासेन तु कौन्तेय वैराग्येण च ग्राह्यते।

But it is conquered by practice and detachment, O son of Kunti.

2. **Set Time Blocks for Deep Work:** Focusing on work without being disturbed is important. It helps the leaders to concentrate and make good decisions. This means no meetings, e-mails, or other things that distract. It is known as "*deep work.*" Doing deep work helps us think better and do high-quality work. By choosing times for this in their days, leaders can show their teams when not to bother them. Doing deep work every day trains our minds to stay on task and get results.
3. **Practice Meditation and Breathwork:** Just taking a few minutes every day to breathe deeply or practice meditatively can go a long way in helping you boost your concentration, as well as your cognitive skills. The mind learns to stay centred thereby removing the mental clutter that hinders the concentration and focus. Dialogue of a few minutes ought to be a daily practice for the boss by which he can excel in the areas of stability and open-mindedness. Breathing exercises, such as controlled inhalation and exhalation, or even activities like jogging, can significantly aid in managing stress and improving mental focus, leading to a calmer state of mind. By incorporating these practices into their daily routines, leaders can cultivate full attention, enabling them to make well-informed strategic decisions and respond to challenges with calmness and clarity.
4. **Follow the 80/20 Rule:** When it comes to boosting productivity, it helps to understand the 80/20 principle. It says that in a majority of situations, around 20% of what we do leads to 80% of what we see as results. This

means that by targeting these, we can become efficient at what we do and increase our efficiency at work. By practicing this rule of focusing on high impact activities, managers can then realign themselves and concentrate on activities that are determined and give results.

5. **Take Breaks Strategically:** Short breathers between demanding work are a powerful way to regain focus and avoid getting worn out. One prevalent belief held by the leading authorities in the corporate world is that continuous work without breaks leads to higher productivity. However, that is not the case. Instead, it frequently brings about mental fatigue and reduced efficiency. Taking short, conscious breaks is a way for the brain to recharge, thus, it will improve concentration and problem-solving. Techniques like the Pomodoro method, that is if people concentrate intensely for a determined period of time, e.g., 25-50 minutes, and then take a short break, can be of a lot of help. When someone takes a small pause in the form of walking, deep breath or stretching mind can be enhanced and, hence, decisions can be made better. A healthy break-time that includes walking sessions will not only refresh the mind but also produce a sound and resultful decision. Leaders can maintain high performance levels and ensure long-term productivity by integrating structured breaks.

Conclusion

Mindfulness and focus are not just spiritual concepts. *They are powerful tools for strategic success.* Leaders who are mindful and well-equipped with these skills will perform better, make sound budgetary decisions and successfully execute their strategies. The Bhagavad Gita's teachings of Dhyana Yoga put forward that the only the capable one is he who has a calm and unwavering mind, it is to let go of attachment as a leader one gets to find the veiled solutions only by the chaste mind.

The final wisdom from the Gita:

"yunjann evam sadatmanam yogi vigata-kalmasah sukhena brahma-samsparsam atyantam sukham asnute"

युञ्जन्नेवमसदात्मानं योगी विगतकल्मषः।
सुखेन ब्रह्मसंस्पर्शमत्यन्तमसुखमाश्नुते॥

Thus, constantly engaging himself, the yogi whose mind is subdued attains the peace that culminates in supreme bliss, in union with the Divine.

A mindful leader tackles obstacles with calm composure, making decisions guided by reason rather than impulse. Mindfulness adds purpose, integrity, and growth to leadership by fostering a culture that is intentional, ethically grounded, and forward-looking. This mindset enhances an organization's effectiveness, adaptability, and capacity for innovation.

Additionally, the centre is of an essential nature to reach organizational strategic goals. In times of many temptations that bombard our mind, it requires the leader to keep minds focused on what really counts. Leaders who take responsibility for their time efficiently rather than giving in to distractions channel their concentrations into tasks that produce the highest return. Adopting mindfulness practices and maintaining narrow focus are strategies that provide executives with benefits such as productivity, decision-making, and courage enhancement.

Mindfulness is a very effective way of transforming the culture of an organization as well. It decreases anxiety, boosts emotional IQ, and enhances relationships among co-workers. A mindful leader proves to be an example for others to follow, thus creates an environment where employees are engaged, feel valued, and believe in what the organization stands for.

To sum it up, authentic leadership is not rather more but is purely about doing what matters with full awareness and purpose. Thus, the entire project can be taken and the proper section can be developed through this. By being focused and full of life, modern leaders are both able to react efficiently in the face of uncertainty and are able to guarantee that their decisions on various strategic moves are not just well-designed but also correctly carried out through strict adhering to the established long-term goals.

CHAPTER 8

Strategic Planning and Execution (Karma Yoga)

Execution is what gives meaning to even the most brilliant strategy. Long-term success belongs to those who can turn vision into action, prioritize effectively, and stay committed to their goals over time. The principle of strategic execution is to conduct business in a selfless manner which is also a Karma Yoga concept in the Bhagavad Gita. Krishna tells Arjuna that one has to be devoted to his duty without thinking of the immediate consequences while performing it. This wisdom is directly related to the strategic planning and execution process that the modern world is witnessing.

A profound shloka in the Gita reminds us:

"karmanye vadhikaraste ma phaleshu kadachana ma karma phala hetur bhurma te sangostva karmani"

कर्मण्येवाधिकारस्ते मा फलेषु कदाचन।
मा कर्मफलहेतुर्भूर्मा ते सङ्गोऽस्त्वकर्मणि॥

You have a right to perform your prescribed duties, but you are not entitled to the fruits of your actions. Never consider yourself to be the cause of the results, and never be attached to not doing your duty.

Successful execution is not based only on a well-planned strategy; it needs discipline, focus, and the capability to overcome obstacles without being distracted by short-term fluctuations. The organizations that fully balance their acts will create a long-term impact and their vision will be a reality made good by proper actions. We see most companies and leaders that end up failing are not because they lack ideas but because they struggle to transform them into action. The ability to stick to the plan, be flexible, and to execute with accuracy is what separates the winning companies from those that fail.

The principle of selfless action tells us that action should be carried out with full dedication, but one should not become too much obsessed with the fruits of action. Leaders should learn how to focus on the process, as they believe in the law of the sustained effort as it will surely bring the desired results. This chapter discusses the ways in which leaders can use the principles of Karma yoga to interrupt the separation between strategy and execution, to select the most important, and to maintain a steadfastness to the goals.

Translating Vision into Action Plans

Vision creates direction and this requires a specific action plan, otherwise, it will remain a vague idea. Many corporations struggle to follow their vision since they have not developed coherent steps that lead to the vision. To be fully implemented, the company has to be organized in the right way which will help them be aligned and responsible for their actions.

The Gita offers wisdom on implementation:

"na hi jnanena sadrisam pavitram iha vidyate tat svayam yoga-samsiddhah kalenatmani vindati"

न हि ज्ञानेन सदृशं पवित्रं इह विद्यते।
तत्स्वयं योगसंपद्धः कालेनात्मनि विन्धति॥

Indeed, there is nothing in this world as purifying as knowledge. One who has become perfect in yoga finds this knowledge within himself in due course of time.

1. Define Clear Objectives

A vision becomes actionable when broken down into clear, achievable objectives for the staff. Management must clarify these objectives by translating broad goals into specific tasks that teams can focus on. For example, instead of stating, "***We want to be the best in our industry***", a company should define success through measurable targets such as market share growth, customer satisfaction scores, or innovation benchmarks.

The purpose of attainable targets is to give a signal to the teams that their efforts have a concrete direction and they help to contribute to the company's broader strategic vision. The clear goals will also enable companies to follow up on their progress, do necessary amendments easily, and keep alignment across the different departments.

2. Develop a Strategic Roadmap

A strategic roadmap steers a team to meet its collective goals. It explains the main projects, the deadlines, the teams in charge, and the resources needed to increase the chance of success. A well-made roadmap is the best assistant, ensuring that the organizations are on track to their vision.

Krishna reminds us about staying focused on the path:

"vyavasayatmika buddhir ekeha kurunandana bahushakha hy anantash ca buddhayo vyavasayinam"

व्यवसायात्मिका बुद्धिर् एकेह कुरुनन्दन।
बहुशाखा ह्यनन्ताश्च बुद्धयो व्यवसिनाम्॥

Those who are on this path are resolute in purpose, and their aim is one. O beloved child of the Kurus, the intelligence of those who are irresolute is many-branched.

Flexibility is an essential quality. A leader should be able to adapt their plans depending on market fluctuations, new opportunities, or any difficulties which come up unexpectedly. The regular checks will keep the roadmap relevant and useful. Organizations can meet the challenges head on and go ahead with a firm conviction by clearly specifying strategy along with the flexibility to alter the plan in case things get complex.

3. Align Teams and Resources

Execution is a collective effort; each department and individual should comprehend their responsibility in the process of strategic goal accomplishment. The transparency and clarity of communication, the training along with resource allocation brings alignment. The work that teams do is more real when people understand the connection it has with the enchanted vision, that is when motivation and work efficiency increase significantly.

Alignment is the first logical step for leaders to define challenges in the workplace. Employees should be fully equipped with the right tools, training opportunities, and resources to perform effectively. Regular check-ins, performance reviews, and open communication channels help keep the team aligned and focused on their goals.

4. Establish Performance Metrics

To keep things moving forward without any problems, the leaders' duty is to delineate the criteria that are measurable. These meters should stamp the progress made within the strategic objectives, thereby giving the teams a chance to adjust their moves. Regular performance reviews help discern pitfalls, and areas for development.

As the Gita teaches:

"samatvam yoga ucyate yogah karmasu kausalam"

समत्वं योग उच्यते योगः कर्मसु कौशलम्॥

Equanimity is called yoga; yoga is skill in action.

The employees are most likely to stay motivated when they can perceive a concrete upgrade and see how their input contributes to the overall output. A review of performance indicators is one thing that a corporation does in the course of time to make their approach even more efficient and to enhance their processes.

Prioritizing Actions for Maximum Impact

A common mistake is the attempt to undertake too many things simultaneously. The most effective leaders and groups concentrate on doing the most important things that will bring about conclusive change. Deciding what is the first thing is a crucial ingredient in time, energy, and resource optimization.

Krishna provides this wisdom:

"saktah karmany avidvamso yatha kurvanti bharata kuryad vidvams tathasaktah cikirsur loka-sangraham"

सक्त: कर्मण्यविधानं यथा कुर्वन्ति भारत।

कुर्याद्विद्वांसतथासक्त: चिकीरिषुरलोकसंग्रहम्॥

As the ignorant perform their duties with attachment, O son of Bharata, so the wise should act without attachment, performing action for the welfare of the world.

1. Apply the 80/20 Rule

The Pareto Principle, known as the 80/20 principle, tells us that 80% of the results come from 20% of the work. Authorities have to separate the principal activities that supply the highest impact and allocate the resources orderly. Through focusing on the most result-oriented endeavours, enterprises achieve the greatest profit and organize their actions in the most efficient way.

To use the Pareto Principle optimally, organizations must analyse their history, find the highest-ranking areas and focus their energy on those tasks that produce the highest value for the organization. The strategy improves productivity, decreases the misuse of energy and guarantees that the teams are dedicated to the main goals.

2. Focus on Core Strengths

Leaders, as well as organizations, need to concentrate on those projects which are in line with their strengths and competitive advantages. The chase after every opportunity leads to dilution of energy, but the commitment to core competencies stands as a sure way to keep the success rate high.

The Gita reminds us:

"sreyan sva-dharmo vigunah para-dharmat sv-anusthitat sva-dharme nidhanam sreyah para-dharmo bhayavahah"

श्रेयान्स्वधर्मो विगुणः परधर्मात्स्वनुष्ठितात्।
स्वधर्मे निधनं श्रेयं परधर्मो भयावहः॥

Better to do one's own duty imperfectly than to do another's duty perfectly. Better to die in one's own duty than to live in another's.

By focusing precisely on their unique strengths, companies can enhance overall effectiveness, maintain their market position, and build long-term value. This targeted approach ensures the judicious use of resources, fostering sustainable and steady growth.

3. Set Short-Term and Long-Term Priorities

By setting short-term milestones that lead towards long-term goals, we can achieve a lot. It's good to have both long, and short-term plans to give us direction and momentum.

Checks in at the end of each week and track progress towards the goals. We can also make changes in tasks using these checks to make everything easier. In today's world of business shifts and surprises, these moves help us to be ready for them.

Long-term goals clarify where we are going over a period of years. They make sure that short-term tasks add up to something big and will still be there in the future. That's when long term goals help everyone be on track and achieve success continually.

4. Leverage Technology and Automation

Technology is capable of automation for replication purposes. Technology empowers teams with the ability to communicate better, get more information and make quicker decisions. Companies effectively using digital tools enjoy more growth and fewer execution challenges.

Krishna speaks about using all available resources:

"yat karosi yad asnasi yaj juhosi dadasi yat yat tapasyasi kaunteya tat kurusva mad-arpanam"

यत्करोषि यदश्नासि यज्जुहोषि दासि यत्।
यत्प्रतस्यसि कौन्तेय तत्कुरुस्व मदार्पणम्॥

Whatever you do, whatever you eat, whatever you offer in sacrifice, whatever you give away, whatever austerity you perform, do that as an offering to Me.

In addition to bringing in project management software, data analytics, and AI-generated reports, a leaders' team can introduce more clear and easy-to-understand decisions to enhance the overall productivity which also results in saving money.

Maintaining Commitment to Strategic Goals

One-time execution is just one part of it. Staying dedicated is a continuous process that lasts months and even years. Many strategies prove ineffective not due to their lack of merit but because in the beginning, they are not as enthusiastic as expected, challenges occur, or conditions change. Real leaders understand that persistence, adaptability, and resilience are the things to focus on for achieving long-term success.

1. Develop a Resilient Mindset

Challenges and downsides are but unavoidable parts in the journey of strategy, and what the leaders do with these setbacks makes or breaks the plans they made. Resilient leaders do not allow quibbles to turn into big problems. Instead, they concentrate on achieving their objectives and plan accordingly.

The Gita offers this wisdom on resilience:

"karmany evadhikaras te ma phalesu kadacana ma karma-phala-hetur bhur ma te sango 'stv akarmani"

कर्मण्येवाधिकारस्ते मा फलेषु कदाचन।
मा कर्मफलहेतुर्भूर्मा ते सङ्गोऽस्त्वकर्मणि॥

You have the right to work only, but never to its fruits. Let not the fruits of action be your motive, nor let your attachment be to inaction.

Having a resilient mindset will help you instil the same in your employees. Visionaries who are always thinking about how they can progress further help seekers of new ways who become innovative, problem-solvers, and agile to come in through identification with the company. They are aware of the fact that missteps are not necessarily negative, but they can help them to get to the real success.

2. Reinforce Purpose and Vision

When goals are clearly defined, teams can fully commit to them and appreciate the positive impact of their efforts. A strong sense of purpose often serves as the driving force that propels people forward, especially during challenging times. Leaders must engage the minds of their employees by clearly explaining the "why" and "how" behind the actions and projects they undertake.

Krishna reminds us about the importance of purpose:

"tasmad asaktah satatam karyam karma samacara asakto hy acaran karma param apnoti purusah"

तस्मादसक्तः सततं कार्यं कर्म समाचर।
असक्तो ह्याचरन्कर्म परमाप्नोति पुरुषः॥

Therefore, without being attached to the fruits of activities, one should act as a matter of duty, for by working without attachment one attains the Supreme.

The visionary executives pass this message through frequent conversations, storytelling, and integration of their core values. They combine the daily piece of work with the main goals thus people feel useful and as if they are the main reason for the success of the company. This is the time when we celebrate the minor victories and sharing the joy of having made it possible ensuring the brigades are aware that they are on the right track.

3. Adapt Without Losing Focus

Adaptability is the real master. In the face of constant conditions, it is important for adapting to a business environment that is in constant change. Markets can change, technology can replace manual work, competition from new competitors can change, and internal dynamics can require new organizations to adjust them to succeed. Nevertheless, you must understand that the adaptation process should neither undermine the core objectives nor the company vision.

As Krishna teaches:

"yat samkhyaih prapyate sthanam tad yogair api gamyate ekam samkhyam ca yogam ca yah pasyati sa pasyati"

यत्सांख्यैः प्राप्यते स्थानं तद्योगैः अपि गम्यते।
एकं संख्यं च योगं च यः पश्यति सः पश्यति॥

What is achieved through analytical understanding can also be attained through dedicated service. One who sees both as one and the same truly sees.

Those companies that win are first of all those that analyse their surroundings continuously, acquire and then apply the knowledge they then have gotten. This is not equal to the company to move from one direction to another but rather to tweak the operations based on the data and challenges that arise.

4. Foster Accountability and Ownership

Commitment to strategic execution is boosted by individuals who take responsibility for their roles and duties. When team members feel particularly engaged with the success of a strategy, retention will be a lot easier and commitment to long-term goals will be possible. Authorities are capable of building such an atmosphere of self-governance by letting people have more space to design within their work scope.

Finding and giving the required recognition also aids efforts to set accountability in stone. Rewarding accomplishments by means of not only appreciation but also through formal recognition or performance incentive plans can highly stimulate retention. Furthermore, the integration of self-reinforcing activities such as team meetings, performance reviews, and clear goal-setting helps to ensure that everyone is on the right course of action with respect to the company's strategic priorities.

5. Celebrate Milestones and Learn from Setbacks

Motivation and engagement are key concepts in any employee's life. This is done when the team reaches the milestones, it is a commitment reinforcement and morale booster. The celebration of victories, however small or large, can bring about a feeling of fulfilment and hence it is an incentive for the employees to put in extra effort towards the company goals.

The Gita teaches about learning from experiences:

"sukha-duhkhe same kritva labhalabhau jayajayau tato yuddhaya yujyasva naivam papam avapsyasi"

सुख-दुःखे समे कृत्वा लाभालाभौ जयजयौ।
ततो युद्धाय युज्यस्व नैवं पापं अवाप्स्यसि॥

Being alike in pleasure and pain, gain and loss, victory and defeat, engage in battle; in this way you will not incur sin.

In the same vein, setbacks should be viewed as steps for learning rather than as endpoints to halt progress or succumb to failure. Instead of yielding to prevailing challenges, leaders should champion a model of continuous growth and development. It is beneficial to discuss the team's difficulties objectively, so the root causes are understood, enabling adjustments to the plan for more effective outcomes.

Conclusion

Discipline, focus, and unwavering commitment to long-term success are basic requirements for strategic planning and execution. A well-formulated strategy on its own does not ensure success; it must be turned into intentional action. The Bhagavad Gita's Karma Yoga teachings are timeless and provide invaluable insights for the leaders who have to deal with the intricacies of implementation.

The final wisdom from the Gita:

"yogasthah kuru karmani sangam tyaktva dhananjaya siddhyasiddhyoh samo bhutva samatvam yoga ucyate"

योगस्थः कुरु कर्माणि संङ्गं त्यक्त्वा धनञ्जय।
सिद्ध्यसिद्ध्योः समो भूत्वा समत्वं योग उच्यते॥

Perform your prescribed duty equipoised, O Arjuna, abandoning all attachment to success or failure. Such equanimity is called yoga.

The core of execution of success is the structured action plans, the prioritizing of high-impact initiatives, and the unwavering commitment to the long-term objectives. At the initial stage, leaders should break goals down into distinct and achievable steps. The educational qualifications, interests, carrying capacities, and skills should be aligned so that employees can move to the successful implementation of the programs.

Execution is not just about doing hardwork. It is about doing smart-work, making data-driven decisions and proposing ideas that will adjust the strategy to fit the challenges. Regardless of this, the first necessity is for leaders to build a culture of accountability, improvement, and innovation which ensures that the team remains motivated and engaged during the process.

A good strategist is not just an idealistic thinker but a hands-on manager who consistently pursues, and attains goals. By implementing the principles of Karma Yoga, leaders form an atmosphere where their strategic plans are not just a product of their imagination but actual, long-term, and grave derivatives. These guided principles will mean leaders will have their strategic rationale to stand the test of time and be remembered for the innovation brought through their execution.

CHAPTER 9

Conflict Resolution

Conflict is an inevitable part of any organization. Whether due to difference of opinion, competing interests, or resource constraints, the elements in employment are there to exploit these differences which can sometimes be damaging. However, conflict is not necessarily a harmful thing. When handled properly and associated with wisdom and ethical fortitude, confrontations or misunderstandings can foster an atmosphere of innovation, forge stronger ties, and promote effective decision-making.

Krishna provides an in-depth treatment of the importance of equanimity when dealing with difficult circumstances in the Bhagavad Gita. The Gita dharma portrays the god advising Arjuna to have a temperate spirit without indulging in mindless emotional fits and irrational beliefs when face-to-face with situations of struggle.

A powerful shloka in the Gita states:

"sukha-duhkhe same kritva labhalabhau jayajayau tato yuddhaya yujyasva naivam papam avapsyasi"

सुख-दुःखे समे कृत्वा लाभालाभौ जयजयौ।
ततो युद्धाय युज्यस्व नैवं पापं अवाप्स्यसि॥

Having made pleasure and pain, gain and loss, victory and defeat the same, engage in battle. In this way you will not incur sin.

From a managerial perspective, leadership is committed to carefully eliminating any problematic tendencies and sharing long term goals harmoniously. Instilling these kinds of values paves way for turning disputes into challenging moments that can help in promoting professional development and more efficient working relationships.

Human beings need to adopt an active and forward-thinking strategy on resolving conflicts; it is a strategy that deals with creating good relations which require communication, respectfulness, and having laid down a process to deal with disputes. There is a need for leaders, who practice Moksha Karma to focus not on the output or personal interest but rather on the development and good for all involved. By doing so, and showing a willingness to address conflict effectively by exploring all the possible options calmly and strategically, high-stake conflicts can come and go without too much damage to the team.

The Yoga of connecting action and partiality as shown in the strategic leaders can use the principles of Karmayoga and the tact of equanimity to handle real-life organizational conflicts properly. It is not only promoting an open and clear atmosphere but also ensuring that everyone is treated equally, so that rifts in communication can be healed and parties can find compromise and resolution. Similarly, when confronted with a possible problem, the fair approach needs to be of calmness by adjustment of the mind. If managed correctly, it is apparent that constructively dealing with conflict has several benefits including trust among employees facilitating cooperation and aiding in attaining common objectives of the organization.

Applying Equanimity in Conflict Management

1. Developing a Calm and Balanced Mindset

Leaders who react impulsively to conflict often escalate tensions rather than resolving them. It is said in the Bhagavad Gita that a person who is wise remains 'sthitaprajna' - steady, and is unaffected by external disturbances. If you want to practice this, then you must approach conflicts with rationality rather than emotion.

The Gita teaches us:

"prajahati yada kaman sarvan partha manogatan atmany evatmana tushtah sthitaprajnas tadocyate"

प्रजाहति यदा कामान् सर्वान् पार्थ मनोगतान्।
आत्मन्येवात्मना तुष्टः स्थितप्रज्ञस्तदुच्यते॥

When one gives up all desires of the mind, O Partha, and becomes satisfied in the self by the self, then he is said to be a person of steady wisdom.

Pause Before Responding: In case of a conflict, it is very helpful to stop for a brief moment and be as impartial as possible when evaluating the entire situation. A peaceful response ensures communication without misunderstandings and exaggerations. Instead of spontaneously becoming emotional, gather the data, take a look from different perspectives, and finally, add the intelligent idea. This satisfaction assures that the discussions won't deviate to blame, but rather remain constructive and to the point of solving the issue.

Practice Active Listening: Conflict resolution can be successful when everyone involved is really listening to each other. If you want to truly understand the other person's perspective, resist the urge to interrupt or think about what to say next. Rather, try to know them first-hand by asking new questions and repeating all the necessary details to be sure that you understand the content. In addition, listening to the other person is one of the ways to find out the main reasons for the problem and also the means to build trust and respect. It is when people feel understood that these are the moments when they most probably will seek for constructive ways of solving problems and ways of cooperation.

Detach from Personal Biases: Effective leaders being human beings, have certain and irregular personal biases. A leader who is free from all the charges exhibits non-partisanship and gives way to these decisions to be made on the grounds of facts, principles, and organization's tasks rather than emotions or personal relations. When supervisors are unbiased in their decisions, they create an environment where elicit trust and cooperation among their subordinates; thus, employees will be more likely to agree with the decisions. The important thing here is for a leader to think about all sides of the situation, to have clear data, and to attempt to make sure the logics behind the resolutions are clear. This process is crucial for the employees to have a sense of getting treated fairly at the workplace.

2. Shifting Focus from Ego to Resolution

The root causes of most of the conflicts are ego-standing quarrels instead of genuine differences in the opinion of people. When the individuals put their personal recognition, pride, or dominance in the first place, the conflicts are extended unnecessarily. The Bhagavad Gita contains the idea of nishkama karma, or selfless action, which in its turn, is the key to focusing on the common good as opposed to personal validation and victory.

Krishna enlightens us with this wisdom:

"karmanye vadhikaraste ma phaleshu kadachana ma karma phala hetur bhurma te sangostva karmani"

कर्मण्येवाधिकारस्ते मा फलेषु कदाचन।
मा कर्मफलहेतुर्भूर्मा ते सङ्गोऽस्त्वकर्मणि॥

You have a right to perform your prescribed duty, but you are not entitled to the fruits of your actions. Never consider yourself the cause of the results of your activities, and never be attached to not doing your duty.

Such leaders embrace the value of humility and, therefore, pursue the resolution of conflicts with fairness and counter arguments instead of merely seeking to justify being right.

Putting aside their ego, these leaders manage to make their workplace collaborative and pleasant to work at. These are some reasons why it's critical for leaders to have a collaborative and comfortable work environment.

Encourage Collaborative Solutions: Disagreements must not be turned into a game of "*who wins who loses*". What the leaders should do instead is to adopt a collaborative approach where all factions join hands together to create win-win solutions. Conflict management, as a concept, becomes a continuum of organization development because of this by providing methods such as open dialogue, mutual understanding, and shared problems to solve conflicts and create innovation and teamwork opportunities.

Address the Issue, Not the Individual: The first and foremost thing required to resolve conflicts is concentrating on the problem instead of the person(s) involved. People who are criticized personally will be too defensive and resentful. By dealing with discussions that are result-oriented, mature, and non-discriminatory, leaders make a base for a positive and consistent conflict resolution which arises from a constructive dialogue.

Cultivate Emotional Intelligence: Emotional intelligence is indeed a cornerstone element in the process of conflict resolution by allowing leaders to stay composed, be aware of others' perspective, and to stay objective. One of the issues one solves by recognizing and managing one's emotions is the prevention of reactive decisions, while viewing things from another's perspective helps in the development of mutual respect among the people. Leaders can now handle conflicts more efficiently and maintain harmony in the workplace by developing such skills as self-awareness, empathy, and patience.

3. Leading by Example

Leaders are the key to the establishment of a good conflict resolution culture which is responsible for extending the progress of organizations. In other words, when they settle disagreements with the most ethical parameters of integrity, fairness, and calmness, they become a benchmark for others to adhere to.

As Krishna teaches:

"yad yad acarati sresthas tat tad evetaro janah sa yat pramanam kurute lokas tad anuvartate"

यद् यद् आचरति श्रेष्ठस् तत्तद् एवेतरो जनः।
स यत् प्रमाणं कुरुते लोकस् तद् अनुवर्तते॥

Whatever action a great man performs, common men follow. Whatever standards he sets by exemplary acts, all the world pursues.

Leaders essentially facilitate constructive conflict resolution by exercising patience, active listening, and impartiality, guiding employees to co-create an environment grounded in respect and collaboration.

Demonstrate Patience and Fairness: Patience and fairness are qualities of leaders who create trust and collaboration in the environment. Listening to different opinions actively, they guarantee that everyone becomes an active player, feels the way they do and has a rapport with their counterparts. Fairness in decision-making which is controlled by facts and not by personal prejudices is the main reason why the leader is viewed as someone worthy of respect and employees are guided by the same principles of respect and rational behaviour. In case if the leaders always behave in this manner, they can build a favourable environment which stimulates relation development and an organization's team spirit and unity.

Stay Solution-Focused: Great leaders know that focusing on problems without looking for solutions only adds to the negativity and frustration. Rather than dwelling on the blame for past mistakes, they steer the conversation toward the search of positive solutions. Being inspired by a forward-looking attitude, they make the team think of practical measures that deal with the source of the conflict. A solution-driven way of working gives the team a proactive and collaborative atmosphere and helps to see challenges as a way of growth, thus making the handling of conflicts to be a way of enacting change rather than standing still.

Promote a Culture of Open Communication: Work environments that foster transparent communication among all stakeholders build trust, collaboration, and accountability, creating the right atmosphere for success. Encouraging employees to voice their concerns early helps prevent misunderstandings and misinterpretations. Effective leaders cultivate a fearless, open, and respectful environment where employees feel safe sharing their views without fear of reprisal. Regular check-ins, open-door policies, and active listening are essential practices to support this culture. When information flows freely and without interference, teams can address issues promptly, leading to a positive and efficient workplace.

Resolving Organizational Conflicts Harmoniously

1. Establishing Clear Conflict Resolution Frameworks

Organizations with established processes for resolving disputes create an equal and systematic way of dealing with conflicts. Through clear principles, they can solve issues immediately and, reduce the probability of an escalation. This not only makes it easier for labourers to work harmoniously but also to make sure that all sides are treated the same way.

Krishna provides this wisdom:

"yogasthah kuru karmani sangam tyaktva
dhananjaya siddhyasiddhyoh samo bhutva
samatvam yoga ucyate"

योगस्थ: कुरु कर्माणि संङ्गं त्यक्त्वा धनञ्जय।
सिद्ध्यसिद्ध्यो: समो भूत्वा समत्वं योग उच्यते॥

Perform your duty equipoised, O Arjuna, abandoning all attachment to success or failure. Such equanimity is called yoga.

Define Conflict Resolution Policies: One of the key factors to consider in order to define the conflict resolution policies in the most effective way is to give specific information. Through these policies, the staff members are guided by specific rules, a situation where a look at it is in the structure and not in the integrity of the rules. Based on these policies, they were developed to be able to settle conflicts transparently and consistently. By describing the steps needed for reporting problems, mediation, or the necessary escalation of the issues, employees become more confident about the matter. The fact that the employees know the process well makes them feel that they can talk things through in a constructive manner because they are aware of the fair and objective way to handle the dispute.

Encourage Mediation: To encourage mediation, it is necessary to bring in a neutral third party to guide the conversation and ensure that both sides have an equal opportunity to present their perspectives. A mediator who is certified, like an HR representative or a senior leader, can contribute to creating a trustworthy and unbiased atmosphere that will calm down the emotional intensity of the situation. In addition to this they are also able to help in identifying common ground, suggest the solutions that may be tried if the resolution is in alignment.

Implement Conflict Training: Conflict training teaches individuals how to solve disagreements well. You learn how to listen, talk calmly and how to see things from other people's point of view including real-life examples. When teams learn conflict-solving, they deal well with problems early on. This makes the workplace better and helps teams work well together. It's less about conflict and more about good problem-solving together.

2. Encouraging Open and Honest Communication

Misunderstandings and misinterpretations are most common reasons during stressful situations. The heads of the companies should promote an atmosphere that is transparent and that it is safe for the mental health of the employees, especially where everyone feels good about airing grievances without the fear of being judged.

The Gita guides us:

"anudvega-karam vakyam satyam priya-hitam ca yat svadhyayabhyasanam caiva van-mayam tapa ucyate"

अनुद्वेग-करम् वाक्यं सत्यं प्रिय-हितं च यत्
स्वाध्यायाभ्यासनं चैव वन्-मयं तप उच्यते॥

Speech that causes no distress, is truthful, pleasant, beneficial, and is used for regular study of scriptures constitutes the austerity of speech.

Open communication with employees helps clarify concerns, prevents assumptions, and enables the resolution of potential issues before they even arise.

Promote Transparency: Transparency in leadership is what creates trust and reduces misunderstandings which could result in conflicts. When bosses disclose their plans, hardships, and make alterations, workers feel given that they are in the loop and recognized rather than feeling ambiguous or left out. The effective transmission of information allows compliance with expectations that ultimately makes everyone realize the whole picture. This honesty also serves as a medium through which employees can share their thoughts and issues openly and easily thus promoting teamwork and interdependency. An environment marked by absolute truth in the workplace finally yields the reverse: no confusion, high integrity and a more united and cognizant organization.

Encourage Constructive Feedback: Promoting positive criticism creates a culture of honesty. Employees find themselves able to air out their minds without getting scared of people's views and fear of negative comments. Respectful transmission and approval of feedback are among the things that can be realized through wise judgment, efficient teamwork, and integration of teamwork at a working place. A good leader thinks about the opinions of the team, takes them into account and deals with problems carefully. A culture that promotes feedback positively leads to trust, employee engagement, and efficiency of organizations as a whole.

Resolve Issues Early: Fixing things early is the main element of a successful and peaceful work environment. Small difficulties, when not fixed right away, can slowly become a major conflict that disrupts teamwork and the mood. Leaders should be the ones to look for and face concerns before they get out of hand and therefore create open communication and timely intervention. By challenging staff members to be brave enough to express their grievances and by providing a resolution system, we can avoid further misunderstandings. Organizations can keep stable, improve relationships, and in the long run provoke synergy by acting swift and thoughtful.

Balancing Interests in Dispute Resolution

1. Fair Decision-Making in Conflicts

Trust building during conflicts is the cornerstone of connection and solidarity within any organization. When resources, promotions, or responsibilities are limited, leaders must handle these challenges with fairness and transparency, rather than personal biases. Clear, open-minded decision-making demonstrates a leader's genuine concern for employees, ensuring they feel valued and treated with honesty.

Krishna offers this wisdom:

"samo 'ham sarva-bhutesu na me dvesyo 'sti na priyah ye bhajanti tu mam bhaktya mayi te tesu capy aham"

समोऽहम् सर्वभूतेषु न मे द्वेष्योऽस्ति न प्रियः।
ये भजन्ति तु मां भक्त्या मयि ते तेषु चाप्यहम्॥

I am equally disposed to all living beings; I am neither inimical nor partial to anyone. But those who render service unto Me with devotion are in Me, and I am in them.

Use Objective Criteria: To make fair decisions and be away from struggles caused by the feeling of being favoured, administrators must be objective and base their judgements on the fact that is measurable, company rules that are explicit, and compliance with organizational objectives not on one's preferences or friendships. The employees trust that the decisions are based on the employee's merits due to the transparency of the decision-making process. Correct, evidence-based decision-making not only decreases disagreements but also promotes an attitude of teamwork that carries responsible and professional behaviours at work.

Be Transparent About Decisions: The leadership should be open about their decision-making by giving all employees the opportunity to be involved in the work that affects their daily duties. The practice of promoting good communication and clear decision-making through trust and elimination of misunderstandings plays a significant role in working relationships within organizations. Therefore, the staff's willingness to hear out farsighted leaders is improved when knowledge is shared in detail. In this respect, transparency is easy to promote and, on the organizational side, the transformation. If bosses can show clearly the prudence of their decisions, they would not only make the process transparent but also increase worker-job satisfaction. Breaking it down further, enhancing total democratic culture and demonstrating servant leadership are vital to employee engagement and development.

Conclusion

While conflict is an undoubted feature of any vibrant organization, it does not necessarily have to be harmful. By mode of the correct conduct, conflict can become an opening to the growth, improvement, and innovation. When wisely handled, fairly, and close to harmony, conflicts are an important source of insights and a window of new inputs. Equanimity, selfless action, and emotional balance, the principles that the Bhagavad Gita has, are helpful tools for leaders to settle differences fulfilled.

The final wisdom from the Gita:

"uddhared atmanatmanam natmanam avasadayet atmaiva hy atmano bandhur atmaiva ripur atmanah"

उद्धरेत् आत्मनात्मानं नात्मानमवसादयेत्।
आत्मैव ह्यात्मनो बन्धुरात्मैव रिपुरात्मनः॥

One must elevate oneself by one's own mind, not degrade oneself. The mind is the friend of the conditioned soul, and the mind is also its enemy.

Culture is one of the most vital building blocks on which a company is founded. Providing access to people's thoughts through open-door communication and other transparent channels creates an environment where employees feel comfortable sharing ideas and concerns. Leaders who handle conflicts with patience and neutrality ensure that everyone's voice is heard, fostering diversity of thought. This approach not only encourages timely solutions but also helps prevent future issues by promoting mutual respect and understanding.

For conflict resolution that is strategic using a "growth mindset" is necessary. The leaders that are committing to the Bhagavad Gita's concepts of balance and selfless action are ideal to be in the workplace. These individuals are those that are striving to reach common goals despite the diversity of views which, in turn, promote unity and produce a stronger organization.

At the end of the day, organizations that are able to deal with conflict effectively will be able to avoid being torn up by differences. On the contrary, these differences are the components of creativity and innovation that in turn bring about the long-term sustainability and success. The businesses by using conflict as a means of spurring the changes of the better can have harmonious environments where shared success is built on the basis of one united front. Collaboration continues to flourish and brings success into companies.

CHAPTER 10

Strategic Human Resource Management

Human Resource Management (*HRM*) is instrumental in any organization not only as a functional department but as a strategic partner in securing long-term business success. In a scenario where businesses are exposed to a larger degree of competitive pressure and rapid change, it starts to become clear that the richest assets of the organization are its people. The problem exists because how to create a common vision that aligns human capital as well as the overall goals of the organization, bringing it in a climate that would naturally allow leadership, motivation, empowerment, and simultaneously ensuring talent is managed for sustainable growth. Drawing conclusions from the timeless implications of the Bhagavad Gita, the HR will be able to act as a major driving force that propels the transformation which the organizations is aiming for.

A profound shloka in the Gita states:

"yatha akasa-sthito nityam vayuh sarvatra-go mahan tatha sarvani bhutani mat-sthanity upadharaya"

यथा आकाशस्थितो नित्यं वायुः सर्वत्रगो महान्।

तथा सर्वाणि भूतानि मत्स्थानीत्युपधारय॥

Just as the mighty wind, blowing everywhere, rests always in the sky, know that in the same manner all beings rest in Me.

The Bhagavad Gita is a philosophical text that deals with duty, leadership, and decision-making and offers the most profound lessons that can help the modern HR. It is to focus the talents to the most influential people and remove the oversight distractions from the whole organization. The teachings of Gita accentuate the significance of perceiving one's part, executing duties with commitment, and nurturing a long-run vision. These qualities are equally pertinent in HR in the corporate world.

Strategic HR management goes far beyond traditional administrative tasks; it involves aligning HR practices with the organization's mission and long-term vision. HR must design policies and processes for recruitment and performance management that address both current business needs and future growth. This includes selecting employees whose values closely align with the company's, fostering leadership at all levels, enhancing employee motivation by emphasizing intrinsic rewards, and empowering teams to take ownership of their work. Additionally, HR should focus on managing human capital to support sustainable growth by ensuring continuous learning and fostering a strong connection between employees and the organization's broader goals.

The chapter is all about the human resource management (HRM) model in which comes up with three main parts that are aligning HR to organizational goals, leadership empowerment and teamwork, and human capital management for long-term success. The combination of these components with the moral foundation given in the Bhagavad Gita will enable HR to create a coherent and strong working team whose activities will ensure the development of the organization and the well-being of the employees in their roles.

Aligning HR Strategy with Organizational Goals

People first must consider the entire organization before they can develop a strategic HR approach. In an episode from the Bhagavad-Gita, Lord Krishna tells Arjuna to focus on the good action and the higher goals without attachment to the results. In the HR landscape, this implies creating strategies that are on the one hand interconnected with the company's mission and on the other hand are the environment for employees to develop themselves.

Krishna teaches this wisdom:

"karmanye vadhikaraste ma phaleshu kadachana ma karma phala hetur bhurma te sangostva karmani"

कर्मण्येवाधिकारस्ते मा फलेषु कदाचन।
मा कर्मफलहेतुर्भूर्मा ते सङ्गोऽस्त्वकर्मणि॥

You have a right to perform your prescribed duties, but you are not entitled to the fruits of your actions. Never consider yourself to be the cause of the results, and never be attached to not doing your duty.

Connecting HR to Organizational Vision

The ability of HR to link to the organization's vision is dependent on how well HR leaders understand the company's fundamental values and long-term goals. This matching is very essential in that it leads to the fact that all HR functions, whether it's hiring talent or training employees, aim to a common goal. In a way, HR professionals see themselves as ancillary to the organization's strategic direction, such is the role of one who brings talent to a company.

To be more specific, for a business that prioritizes innovation and continuous development in its vision, HR should focus on the talent acquisition process that looks for creative workers who are adaptable and who can work in a fast-paced environment. These will not just be a fit for the company culture but also be the people who will actively participate in the company's growth and innovation process. Here, HR can be on the lookout for candidates with a reputation of problem-solving, with entrepreneurial thinking, and who are eagerly into new ideas.

In a similar fashion, when exceptional customer service is the primary motivation, HR should prioritize recruitment criteria that emphasize interpersonal skills, empathy, and a genuine desire to help others. Training and development programs must be tailored to continuously enhance employees' customer service capabilities and ensure their behavior aligns with the organization's vision of delivering outstanding experiences. This strong integration between HR practices and the corporate mission fosters a motivated, engaged workforce united in pursuing shared goals.

Recruitment and Talent Acquisition

Recruitment and the acquisition of talent are basics to the harmony between HR and the company's overall objectives. Instead of concentrating solely on vacant spots to be filled, HR should strategically recruit applicants as well as making sure that each staff member accepting the job embodies the company's values, culture, and long-term vision.

As Krishna teaches:

"sreyan sva-dharmo vigunah para-dharmat sv-anusthitat sva-dharme nidhanam sreyah para-dharmo bhayavahah"

श्रेयान् स्वधर्मो विगुण: परधर्मात्स्वनुष्ठितात्।
स्वधर्मे निधनं श्रेयो परधर्मो भयावह:॥

It is better to perform one's own duties imperfectly than to perform another's duties perfectly. Better to die in one's own duty than to live performing another's duty.

The Bhagavad Gita teaches Arjuna to align his actions with a higher purpose beyond immediate outcomes. Similarly, HR professionals must ensure that the individuals they recruit are not only qualified but also share the organization's mission and core values. This alignment fosters a workforce committed to the broader vision, strengthening both individual and organizational growth.

For example, when a firm's goal mentions innovation, the HR recruiting plan should give priority to the people who are not only talented but also who are enthusiastic about the change and are bringing innovative views to the firm. Such candidates would do well in a workplace that promotes creativity and critical thinking. In contrast, for an organization that is community-oriented or customer excellence service-oriented, HR should pick individuals who have exemplary communication skills, empathy, acquaintance, and sincere eagerness for making a good impact on others.

HR attracts people who are motivated and devoted to contributing to the organization's larger objectives by ensuring this alignment. This in turn builds a workforce that is not only skilled but also engaged and committed to the success of the company.

Training and Development

Employee education and training are the key to the creation of a right balance between human capital and organizational objectives. Once the employees are hired, HR has to assure that they have got learning, knowledge, and positive attitude so that they will be beneficial to the company's mission.

The Bhagavad Gita's teachings by Krishna point out the significance of the constant development of one's own self and the search for basic wisdom, which is integral to HR approaches to employee development. Just as Arjuna is advised by Krishna to develop and expand, HR should ensure that each employee receives enough opportunities for learning thus enlightening them to accomplish the highest performance in the workplace.

HR needs to devise training programs that are broader in scope and that involve the long-term development of the organization. Such activities may include training personnel to occupy leadership positions in the future and the capacity of skills such as decision-making, strategic thinking, and emotional intelligence. Apart from that, training, learning, and development that occur through workshops, online courses, and collaboration in different departmental can help keep employees passionate and highly gladdened in a rapidly mutating business environment.

The promotion of mentoring activities will also aid in matching the staff with the organizational objectives. The connection between experienced senior leaders and budding talent allows HR to transfer information, give them direct instructions, and in the process the HR staff develops the corporate culture.

Leadership, Motivation, and Team Empowerment

Leadership stands at the forefront of an organization's success, and the Bhagavad Gita offers profound insights into how leaders can guide, inspire, and motivate their teams toward achieving goals. The leadership exemplified by Lord Krishna is rooted in empathy, wisdom, and the ability to inspire purposeful action. By embracing these values, HR can cultivate a leadership culture that resonates deeply and is embraced by everyone within the organization.

Transformational Leadership

In the Bhagavad Gita, Krishna is the perfect model of transformational leadership helping Arjuna to embrace his duty and reach his higher purpose. Krishna does not just tell Arjuna what to do but rather helps him to act with confidence, wisdom, and self-awareness.

That is the core of transformational leadership - managers who inspire and motivate their teams to do better and lead them to the same objectives. In the same way, HR leaders should awaken transformational leadership by creating an environment of growth, innovation, and collaboration, where leaders are urged to expose their hidden potential.

This is where HR is a leading actor because they develop the leader's effectiveness through programs that focus on self-awareness, emotional intelligence, and strategic thinking. For instance, like Arjuna who is guided by Krishna, HR should design leadership development programs that enable individuals to grow, develop new skills and lead their teams with purpose and clarity.

Charismatic leaders not only guide their teams, but they help them find their areas of expertise and thus, they are able to innovate, collaborate, and exceed beyond expectations. HR has to identify future leaders, coach, mentor, and prepare them for such leadership roles to venture the journey of personal change and enable their team to adopt such a method smoothly. This action is an important one for HR, since it will, in turn, enable the workforce to relate to the organization's vision and values and thus align it.

Motivation Through Intrinsic Rewards

Krishna advises Arjuna to focus on selfless action, performing duties without attachment to the outcomes. In a company setting, this translates to inspiring employees through intrinsic rewards—such as a strong sense of purpose, personal and professional growth, and fulfillment in their work—rather than relying solely on external incentives.

Krishna reminds us:

"svalpam apy asya dharmasya trayate mahato bhayat"

स्वल्पमप्यस्य धर्मस्य त्रायते महतो भयात्।

Even a small amount of this dharma protects one from great fear.

This can be carried out by:

1. **Recognition and Praise:** It is important to be aware of how employee engagement and motivation can be boosted by using recognition and praises. Frequent acknowledgements given to the employees about their

contributions to the firm can make them feel that they are valued and that they are committed to the organization they work for. Nonetheless, it is important that the recognition be given from the heart and it has to be connected to the performance directly. The value of the praise will be lost if there is no visible connection between the commendations and the employee's achievements. A good recognition program will highlight not only the individual works of the employees but also their skills and accomplishments and, therefore, it will make it clear to them that their contributions are along the company's goals.

2. **Opportunities for Growth:** One of the most important things when it comes to promoting motivation and loyalty among employees is the provision of opportunities for growth. In the course of the organization's life, employees will be more motivated and will stay enthusiastic if there is a clear growth path showing them that they can invest in their assignments. Imagine a model where individuals enjoy unlimited access to training programs, dynamic leadership development initiatives, and exciting opportunities for departmental transfers. This approach not only empowers personal growth but also fosters a vibrant culture of continuous learning and career advancement!. Involving workers in the promotion of their careers and teaching them new skills for success is enough to make them feel important and be motivated as they are the ones who are in high demand. As a result, they will have a good relationship with the company, which is expressed in the increased level of engagement, a good

degree of job satisfaction, and a long-term mutually beneficial rapport.

The fact of the matter is that motivation doesn't have to only be based on them getting a bonus or a pay raise, perhaps another and better strategy is to develop an environment, which would otherwise incite the employees to their roles more effectively that will make them intrinsically motivated.

Empowering Teams

Empowering teams to foster a culture of trust and collaboration is essential. Duty and accountability, key principles highlighted in Krishna's guidance to Arjuna, are foundational in this process. For HR professionals, this means ensuring that employees are equipped with the necessary resources, given the authority, and entrusted with the responsibility to make decisions within their roles.

Team empowerment can be achieved by:

Delegating Decision-Making Power: One effective way to actively involve your staff and encourage them to be more responsible is through the delegation of authority to teams. When employees have the responsible leadership skills to handle issues themselves, they are encouraged and get a chance to be further recognized by the organization, gaining a deeper sense of liability. Consequently, the inclusion of people results in expected outcomes where the workers are even motivated to bring out their very best and thus contribute positively to the team in turn. Also, there are higher chances that the teams which are empowered to make decisions are more inclined to be problem-solvers and to be creative and more flexible. In this way, it also fortifies the relation between an employee and an employer, hence it can improve also emotional occupations and the wellbeing of a company.

Encouraging Autonomy: Autonomy in the workplace can be a good way to inspire imagination and innovation. When employees are allowed to be more creative and independent, they can take risks, explore their new creative ideas, and be able to have the confidence to decide which improves their self-esteem. It allows employees to see innovations as they are not ex situ. They are also given freedom to come up with unique resolutions that would not otherwise be voiced. Also, when employees are empowered and trusted to take initiative, they become more motivated and the success of the company becomes their own success. By establishing a culture where independence is the key element, businesses can nurture a culture of innovation, accountability, and continuous improvement.

Krishna guides Arjuna into battle with unwavering resolve, inspiring him to confront challenges with determination and courage. In a similar manner, the HR professional plays a crucial role in guiding employees through the complexities of their work environment, fostering a strong belief in their abilities and potential. This dual guidance not only strengthens spirits but also empowers individuals to reach their highest potential.

Managing Human Capital for Long-Term Success

In the Bhagavad Gita, Krishna explains that to achieve the goal of success at work, you have to work the hardest, persevere through the bad days, see the big picture (goal), and never quit no matter how hard and bleak the present is.

Krishna shares this wisdom:

"tasmad asaktah satatam karyam karma samacara asakto hy acaran karma param apnoti purusah"

तस्मादसक्तः सततं कार्यं कर्म समाचर।

असक्तो ह्याचरन् कर्म परमं आप्नोति पुरुषः॥

Therefore, without being attached to the fruits of activities, one should act as a matter of duty, for by working without attachment one attains the Supreme.

Human Resource management must adopt a similar approach when overseeing the workforce—focusing not only on immediate needs but also on sustaining a resilient and sustainable workforce over time. Simply recruiting and training employees is not enough; HR must develop long-term strategies that actively engage employees, cultivate loyalty, and ensure continuous growth.

Continuous Development and Growth

In the Bhagavad Gita, Krishna explains that to achieve the goal of success at work, you have to work the hardest, persevere through the bad days, see the big picture (*goal*), and never quit no matter how hard and bleak the present is. Human Resource must be this way too when administering the workforce, taking care not just of the immediate but of the maintenance of a sustainable workforce as well. Just recruiting and training are insufficient; HR needs to develop long-term strategies that engage employees, foster loyalty, and guarantee continuous growth.

HR should implement:

1. **Ongoing Training Programs:** It is very important to carry out ongoing training programs in order to keep

everyone engaged and their skills updated. In providing non-stop professional development chances, the organization gives the employees the possibility to keep up with industry trends, acquire new skills, and at the same time, adapt to the constantly changing business requirements. This learning investment promotes the growth of individual and the achievement of the organization in a dynamic environment.

2. **Career Pathing:** The need for career pathing is vital for the success of employee motivation and retention. Better Human Resources should be involved in the creation of these well-articulated and systematic career paths that are consistent with the organization's long-term objectives and at the same time offering a personal growth opportunity. By giving them a roadmap for advancement, employees become more motivated and are more likely to align themselves with company goals, thereby improving both engagement and loyalty to the company occupation.

Employee Retention and Commitment

Throughout the Bhagavad Gita, Krishna tells the importance of adhering to duty and being fully devoted to the task at hand. The case is the same with human resources which has to work hard to materialize a culture of loyalty and commitment in the workplace. The retention strategies must aim at wants not only in the way of money, but also for employees to feel like a part of something, to love it and to feel supported by the company.

Krishna advises:

"yuktah karma-phalam tyaktva santim apnoti naisthikim ayuktah kama-karena phale sakto nibadhyate"

युक्तः कर्मफलं त्यक्त्वा शान्तिं आप्नोति नैष्ठिकीम्।

आयुक्तः कामकारेण फले सक्तो बन्ध्यते।

One who works in devotion, who is a pure soul, and who controls his mind and senses, is dear to everyone, and everyone is dear to him. Though always working, such a person is never entangled.

Effective employee retention strategies include:

Recognizing and Rewarding Loyalty: Giving importance to long-term employees and rewarding them will be beneficial to customer retention and loyalty. HR departments will thank these employees by recognizing their hard work, maybe by giving such awards as the best or the most detailed or by giving them a special participation in a company event and propose them for a reposition. Allowing employees to work from home part-time gives them more balance between their professional and personal lives. By honouring them, which is an important value, companies strengthen employee dedication and make them feel that they need to take part in the company's success.

Fostering a Positive Work Environment: Creating a positive work environment is an essential factor for employee satisfaction and retention. In the process of building a supportive, inclusive, and respectful culture, organizations mark their footsteps in the workplace, which gives the employees a feeling of significance and motivation to work. Such work involves the young generation in the process of workforce management-by the way, the automotive industry needs this kind of activity. With teamwork, open communication, and mutual respect as the base, the gain of trust is also a profit for both loyalty as well as for overall organizational success.

Conclusion

To effectively align human resources with the overarching vision and objectives of an organisation, it is essential to focus on strategic hiring and clear responsibilities. This approach fosters a culture in which HR is integrated into the organisation's goals, enhancing overall effectiveness and support for achieving targets. Like every department is a lever for the company, HR is a mechanism for the development of the motivated, committed, and high-performing workforce. A good HR policy arrangement makes sure that workers are not only working for the company but rather actively contributing to its mission.

The final wisdom from the Gita:

"sarva-dharmān parityajya mām ekaṃ śaraṇaṃ vraja ahaṃ tvāṃ sarva-pāpebhyo mokṣayiṣyāmi mā śucaḥ"

सर्वधर्मान्परित्यज्य मामेकं शरणं व्रज।
अहं त्वां सर्वपापेभ्यो मोक्षयिष्यामि मा शुचः॥

Abandon all varieties of dharma and just surrender unto Me. I shall deliver you from all sinful reactions. Do not fear.

A key element of strategic HR management is alignment. When HR functions—such as recruitment, training, and development—are fully integrated with the company's vision, employees gain a clear understanding of their role within the organization's broader mission. This alignment inspires employees to find purpose in their work and fosters their commitment to collaborate in achieving shared goals.

Additionally, HR must evolve by cultivating transformational leadership, empowering leaders to inspire, support, and guide their teams toward innovative, collaborative, and long-term success.

Belief is yet another decisive issue. Motivation, when practiced by HR through the means of recognition, growing opportunities, and a friendly working atmosphere, can lead to a high level of employee engagement. Correspondingly, the strategic management of the human resources through general performance feedback, career development plans, and continuous learning, as well as improvement of the managerial skills of employees so that they can grow with the organization, is an element that must be used.

Taking this as an example, just as Lord Krishna supported and guided Arjuna with knowledge and a lot of light, HR leaders should provide their teams with vision purpose and most importantly support. Through such integration, HR ensures that companies are not only surviving the challenges of the difficult business world of today but are able to create a committed, enthusiastic, and dedicated workforce that works towards long-term success.

CHAPTER 11

Team Building and Collaboration

In today's business world, the path to success is not always a lonely one. A great team of people is the foundation of the rest of the elements, such as innovation, efficiency, and sustainability. A well-coordinated team not only enhances productivity but also promotes a strong work culture where the members are both satisfied and motivated. Ancient Indian wisdom offers profound insights into leadership, unity, and collective purpose all of which are pertinent to team building and collaboration in contemporary organizations.

A beautiful shloka states:

"ekaki na tu gaccheta na ca supte jane vrajeta eko hi bahudha bhutva lokams caraty acintyatma"

एकाकी न तु गच्छेथा: न च सुप्ते जाने व्रजेत्।
एको हि बहुधा भूत्वा लोकान् चरत्य अचिन्त्यात्मा॥

One should not walk alone, nor journey while others sleep. For the mysterious soul, though appearing as one, becomes many and moves through all worlds.

This ancient wisdom reminds us that collaboration is key and it is the foundation for success and focus. Every individual has a specific role in the big picture and only through their genuine commitment and hard work, the whole community can benefit. This concept is of course consistent with today's team dynamics, where each participant's input, making the team whole.

A high-performance team is more than just a collection of talented individuals; it is a unified whole built on trust and synergy. True cohesion arises from mutual trust, shared responsibility, and a common vision. When team members clearly understand their roles and feel genuinely connected to the group, the team's overall impact strengthens, and collaborative efficiency significantly improves.

This chapter will focus on the methods for creating a high-performance team, which include the cooperation of the employees, the full respect of the workers towards each other and the joint access to the same goal through mutual respect.

Building High-Performance Teams

It is not every day that we witness the addition of a few participants to the organization who will take up the challenge of accelerating the growth of the workshop and the quality of content. Ancient Indian principles speak about the concept of duty, and the concept of selfless action without which teamwork becomes an impossibility.

A famous shloka teaches:

"samgatam sampravadante samgatam ca parasparam asato jnanam utpannam samgatam pravadanti tat"

संगतं संप्रवदन्ते संगतं च परस्परम्।
असतो ज्ञानम् उत्पन्नं संगतं प्रवदन्ति तत्॥

Those who come together, speak together and engage with one another - from their interactions, knowledge arises. This is the benefit of coming together.

1. Defining Roles and Responsibilities

In every group, each person must have a clear understanding of his role and how it can help to achieve the overall objective. In the same way that ancient wisdom encouraged warriors to regard their duty, management should also make sure each team member knows his job details and is eager to fulfil them.

Clearly set roles mean there is no ambiguity and thus the employees do not need to put the same effort repeatedly. Furthermore, when every employee knows their responsibilities, they will be more productive and will also take responsibility for their work. The leaders are the ones who have to set guidelines for the employees and ensure that individual roles are aligned with the organization's goals. Regular check-ins and feedback sessions can help the team members remain on schedule and adapt to shifting priorities.

2. Selecting the Right People

Building an effective team largely depends on selecting individuals who not only possess the necessary skills but also align with the company's core values. While skills can be developed over time, it is attitude, adaptability, and the ability to work well with others that form the true foundation for long-term success.

The shloka offers this wisdom:

"vidya vivadaya dhanam madaya shaktih pareshaam paripidanaaya khalasya sadhor viparitam etat jnanaya danaya ca rakshanaya"

विद्या विवादाय धनं मदाय

शक्तिः परेषां परिपीडनाय।

खलस्य साधोर्विपरीतमेतत्

ज्ञानाय दानाय च रक्षणाय॥

For the wicked, knowledge leads to arguments, wealth to pride, and power to harming others. For the good person, these same things lead to wisdom, charity, and protection.

The success of a company is not solely based on the evaluation of resumes and technical qualifications. Companies should place an emphasis on those that exhibit a collaborative mindset and demonstrate that they are eager to acquire new knowledge and are ready to take responsibilities. The staff members who share the same company's vision and culture are more likely to create a positive working environment and success in the team of both dynamics and overall achievements.

3. Encouraging Accountability

Ancient texts talk about the importance of doing the job that is assigned to you with your whole being, yet not worrying about the outcome. The idea of remaining objective and detached is a significant habit that can lead to good teamwork that relies on individual accountability for success.

A shloka reminds us:

"uttisthata jagrata prapya varan nibodhata ksurasya dhara nisita duratyaya durgam pathas tat kavayo vadanti"

उत्तिष्ठत जाग्रत प्राप्य वरान्निबोधत।
क्षुरस्य धारा निशिता दुरत्यया
दुर्गं पथस्तत्कवयो वदन्ति॥

Arise, awake, and learn by approaching the excellent ones. The path is difficult to traverse, like the sharp edge of a razor, so say the wise.

Promoting accountability within a team cultivates mutual trust and respect. Each individual is not only responsible for completing their own tasks but also committed to contributing equally toward the team's collective goals. When team members embrace responsibility, they are empowered to take initiative, lead proactively, and fulfill their duties fueled by the shared mission that unites them.

Fostering Collaboration and Synergy

True collaboration is not always easy to achieve, but when it happens, it creates synergy—where the team's combined efforts produce results greater than the sum of individual contributions. Ancient wisdom highlights the importance of unity and harmony as essential foundations for effective teamwork.

This shloka beautifully expresses:

"sam gacchadhvam sam vadadhvam sam vo manamsi janatam deva bhagam yatha purve sanjanana upasate"

सं गच्छध्वं सं वदध्वं सं वो मनांसि जानताम्।
देवा भागं यथा पूर्वे संजनाना उपासते॥

Walk together, speak together, let your minds understand as one. Just as the ancient gods sharing their portion remain united.

1. Creating a Shared Vision

A shared vision is the nucleus of any high-performance team because it offers a direct path and a reason for the people to come together. A good vision provides a foundation for determining team member performance, since it focuses on the scope of their work in the whole endeavor.

The great art of leadership is in the power to dream things and in turn making those dreams come alive through the efforts of their group members as well. Clearly listing a motive is not only energizing but it is a building block of joint success, since every person knows that their effort is a part of a bigger picture. A unified vision made strong can keep a team on track and ensure good cohesion enabling it to weather the storms and still stay focused with the pressure.

2. Encouraging Mutual Support

Encouraging mutual support is extremely important for the formation of a strong and cohesive team. The chapter from the Mahabharata with Pandavas as its heroes is a story of loyalty and devotion, where they are practically inseparable in their provision of mutual backing in all the trials they undergo.

This shloka teaches us:

"yatheha sarve prajananti tatha kurvantu nityada anyonyasya vyatikramam na kuryur hitakamyaya"

यथेह सर्वे प्रजानन्ति तथा कुर्वन्तु नित्यदा।
अन्योन्यस्य व्यतिक्रमं न कुर्युर् हितकाम्यया॥

As all know here, so should all always act. For their mutual benefit, let none transgress against another.

The bond between the team members stood the test of time, enabling them to overcome numerous challenges and exemplify the core principle of strength in unity. A team thrives when its members willingly engage in work driven by a shared mission—one that values collaboration over competition and fosters a positive, supportive environment rather than toxicity.

Leaders must cultivate a culture where lifting each other up is clearly valued—whether through celebrating collective achievements or offering support during difficult times. These shared victories build a strong sense of togetherness, reinforcing that success is a collective effort and that everyone benefits from a spirit of community and mutual respect.

Achieving Unity of Purpose through Mutual Respect

One of the main keys to effective cooperation is respect from both sides. According to ancient wisdom, being modest and respectful to the others are the first steps to wisdom and productive teamwork. Through this mutual understanding, the team members are able to communicate openly, trust, and cooperate, thereby, the relationships are strengthened and this eventually leads to the success of the collective team.

This shloka offers this wisdom:

"Sarve bhavantu sukhinah, sarve santu niramayah;
Sarve bhadrani pashyantu, ma kashchit duhkha bhag bhavet."

सर्वे भवन्तु सुखिनः सर्वे सन्तु निरामयाः।
सर्वे भद्राणि पश्यन्तु मा कश्चिद्दुःखभाग्भवेत्॥

It means, may all be happy, may all be free from illness. May all see auspiciousness, may none suffer in sorrow.

1. Respecting Diverse Perspectives

Form of respect for diverse perspectives is of a prime importance for promoting originality and helping teams make the best possible decision. Ancient wisdom highlights the fact that solving problems is facilitated much easier when one can look at different perspectives on things, rather than be limited to one's own point of view.

Greater mutual respect results in a more open conversation and critical thinking or, in other words, team members can examine a wider variety of ideas. Open debates serve as a catalyst for disruption, compelling individuals to broaden their perspectives and explore innovative ideas. Alternatively, they may increasingly gravitate toward mainstream beliefs at an accelerated pace, fostering a heightened tolerance for deliberate changes and inviting fresh discussions on established norms. Thus, diversity becomes an effective tool for not only increasing the creativity but also the decision making it a powerful instrument for the team's success.

2. Leading by Example

Leadership is a crucial factor in enhancing team performance. The way team members treat, cooperate, and overcome difficulties is all set by the leaders. When the leaders show respect, humility, and a strong dedication to the team's vision, they not only influence the others to accept these ideas but also take them on by themselves.

A famous shloka says:

"yatha sarvani bhutani dhara dharyate sama tatha sarvani bhutani bibhratah parthivam vratam"

यथा सर्वाणि भूतानि धरा धार्यते समा।

तथा सर्वाणि भूतानि बिभ्रत: पार्थिवं व्रतम्॥

Just as the earth supports all beings equally, so should a leader support all people without discrimination.

Leading by positive example is the most powerful way for management to shape a team's culture and behavior. A leader's humility creates an environment where team members feel recognized and are comfortable sharing their ideas without fear of criticism. When the leader diligently monitors the group's goals, it inspires members to elevate their efforts toward a higher purpose, ensuring everyone works together toward a shared vision.

Conclusion

Ancient Indian wisdom is a very forceful expression of the essence of unity, collaboration, and common purpose, which are the bedrock requirements for a team to succeed. The wisdom passed down through generations is the equivalent of the saying that might makes right when it is realized through the work of disciplined individuals reaching the same goal.

A famous shloka reminds us:

"nayam atma pravacanena labhyo na medhaya na bahuna srutena yameva esa vrnute tena labhyas tasyaisa atma vivrnute tanum svam"

नायमात्मा प्रवचनेन लभ्य:

न मेधया न बहुना श्रुतेन।

यमेवैष वृणुते तेन लभ्यः
तस्यैष आत्मा विवृणुते तनूं स्वाम्॥

This Self is not attained through instruction, nor through intellect, nor through much learning. It is attained by the one whom the Self chooses; to such a one the Self reveals its own nature.

In the line of organizational leadership, this message stands out bright—it is critical for the leaders to foster a communicative environment that welcomes the team members to work in a coordinated manner and so teaming is the key-players must understand the need for collaboration and their role in contributing to the collective vision.

Creating high-performance teams is not just about personal accomplishment; it is about the environment of synergy being established, where cooperation is underscored above all things. Synergy happens when the input of the team is higher than the aggregate result of the individuals and it promises more creativity, innovation, and problem-solving. The primary motive here is mutual respect. Where members are respected and valued for their distinctive views and skills, their interest in the task and motivation will be greatly increased.

As ancient wisdom encourages, leaders should bestow their teams a clear vision, directive, and support. Through communicating an agreed-upon aim and building a trusting environment with all team members, leaders can shape such teams that are talented, resilient, and guarantee long-term success.

CHAPTER 12

Stakeholder Management

The efforts of stakeholders form the foundation of a leader's success, especially in today's unstable business environment. Modern organizations are complex networks of relationships involving numerous stakeholders—employees, customers, investors, suppliers, local communities, regulatory bodies, and more. Each group brings its own interests, expectations, and demands, which can sometimes conflict with one another. One of the key challenges that leaders face is balancing these competing interests effectively.

A profound verse states:

"sarve gunaah kaanchanam aashrayanti daanaaya shaurya pranatirbhavaya praapya dhanam yan na dadati paatre tasya dhanam viphalam jivitam cha"

सर्वे गुणाः काञ्चनम् आश्रयन्ति

दानाय शौर्यं प्रणतिर्भवाय।

प्राप्य धनं यन् न ददाति पात्रे

तस्य धनं विफलं जीवनं च॥

All virtues reside in gold - it can be given in charity, it lends courage, and it promotes humility. If one obtains wealth and does not give to the deserving, both wealth and life are in vain.

The wisdom of ancient texts illustrates philosophical ideas that are of the utmost importance in terms of many aspects of human life, such as decision-making processes, relationships, and responsibilities. In spite of the fact that these texts were created thousands of years ago, their principles are really topical in contemporary leadership dilemmas. They are based on the theory of righteous conduct: the righteous path that is implanted in the laws of morality and which becomes an individual's guiding principle for his actions.

Stakeholder management which is a concept of the harmonizing of individual actions with the common welfare is very important in stakeholder management. The very first task of leaders is making the decisions that will affect a broad range of stakeholders. Leaders ought to be able to carefully consider the needs and interests of all the parties involved whether they are deciding on resource allocation, resolving conflicts, or setting organizational policies.

This chapter will be devoted to how these timeless lessons can be used for stakeholder management. We will see the connection of the concepts of balancing stakeholder demands, ethical decision-making, and engaging stakeholders strategically to these ancient teachings, which, in turn, can be transformed into leaders who can acquire wisdom and integrity of character with the challenges of modern leadership.

Balancing Stakeholder Interests Ethically

Ethical balancing of stakeholders' interests is a chief problem for any higher-up. Different stakeholders, such as workers, customers, shareholders, and the greater community, often have divergent priorities and outlooks. For example, employees might be the ones asking for higher wages or better working conditions, while the investors may have their focus on the reduction of costs and profitability.

This verse offers this wisdom:

"sukhasya mulam dharmah dharmasya mulam arthah arthasya mulam rajyam rajyasya mulam indriyajayah"

सुखस्य मूलं धर्मः
धर्मस्य मूलं अर्थः
अर्थस्य मूलं राज्यम्
राज्यस्य मूलं इन्द्रियजयः॥

The root of happiness is dharma (righteousness), the root of dharma is artha (economic prosperity), the root of artha is governance, and the root of governance is self-control.

1. The Importance of Fairness and Transparency

Transparency and fairness are the two basic principles that are essential for effective leadership and decision-making, especially in the of the situation which involves various stakeholders. In business, the leaders of the organizations have to make certain decisions which calcify the necessities of the employees, the clients, the investors, and the other stakeholders among themselves.

Ancient wisdom provides precious knowledge on this subject. It advises leaders to actualize their self-interest by benefitting not only society but the world with their actions. This perspective is single because it is beyond selfish interests and forklifts the leaders to a broader moral plane. Furthermore, fairness in the case of decision-making amongst the leaders always results in establishing the trust and recognition of their teams and groups.

2. Ethical Decision-Making and Its Impact on Trust

Ethical decision-making is a crucial tool for achieving long-term success, whether in developing accommodations or managing stakeholder relationships. When leaders base their decisions on ethical principles, their messages to staff and stakeholders become clear—demonstrating honesty, fairness, and integrity.

This verse reminds us:

"satyam bruyat priyam bruyat na bruyat satyam apriyam priyam cha nanritam bruyat esha dharmah sanatanah"

सत्यं ब्रूयात् प्रियं ब्रूयात्
न ब्रूयात् सत्यं अप्रियम्।
प्रियम् च नानृतं ब्रूयात्
एष धर्मः सनातनः॥

Speak the truth, speak what is pleasant. Do not speak the truth which is unpleasant, and do not speak pleasant falsehoods. This is the eternal law.

For instance, leaders who can probe into the overall outcome of their acts to understand how the decisions affect the employees, customers, investors, and even the whole community, provide a sense of value and respect for those stakeholders. The trustful environment results in better outcomes due to the higher self-interest of the constituents who are more likely to work together.

Also, ethical decision-making through openness of information in which stakeholders understand the logic behind the decisions causes the reduction of ambiguity and a bolstering of goodwill. Transparency warrants that no sector eludes sustaining the betterment of the whole and functional/efficiency of the organization.

Upholding Right Conduct in Decision-Making

Ancient wisdom focuses on righteous duty as a major guiding principle in the choices making procedure. Righteous duty induces people to behave in sync with their higher duties - even if it means sacrificing the pleasure that they get from their exclusive desires, fears, or attachments to things.

The Mahabharata shares this guidance:

"ahimsa satyam akrodha tyagah shantir apaishunam daya bhuteshu aloluptvam mardavam hrir achapalam"

अहिंसा सत्यं अक्रोधः
त्यागः शान्तिरपैशुनम्।
दया भूतेष्वलोलुप्त्वं
मर्दवं ह्रीरचापलम्॥

Non-violence, truthfulness, freedom from anger, renunciation, tranquillity, aversion to fault-finding, compassion for all beings, freedom from covetousness, gentleness, modesty, and absence of fickleness.

Integrity, impartiality, and a commitment to the common good are qualities cultivated through such work. Therefore, decisions should not only serve the organization's primary stakeholders but also uphold the broader interests of the organization itself. This approach fosters trust and strengthens ethical leadership.

1. Understanding Right Conduct as a Leadership Principle

If a person wants to keep the company consensus as his or her pointer, right conduct is of utmost importance. Right conduct, quite simply, is doing your duty in an upright and ethical way, no matter how much your own desires are or be external forces. To this end, the primary aim of leaders is to make choices that help the organization and its various stakeholders, even though the decisions are not the quickest and most profitable in the near future.

Leaders who follow right conduct think very differently about what is gained in terms of the good of everyone than private gain or immediate rewards do. They lead in decisions that are just, fair, and that are in line with the organization's values and mission, even when these choices may be difficult or unpopular.

By doing right, leaders later establish trust in the company and with the outside groups such as customers, investors, and workers. People that may want to choose people that are honest with their ethical behaviour are customers, as they are impressive that the decisions are made with their interest at heart, rather than the ones that are advantaged.

2. Aligning Business Practices with Righteous Duty

A famous shloka advises:

yatra yatra ratiḥ satyā na tatra mithyā sambhavet
yatra mithyā pravṛttis tu na tatra satyam ucyate

यत्र यत्र रतिः सत्या
न तत्र मिथ्या संभवेत्।

यत्र मिथ्या प्रवृत्तिः तु
न तत्र सत्यम् उच्यते॥

Wherever love is true, falsehood cannot exist. Wherever there is deceit, truth has no place.

Falsehood may be easy to embrace, but once practiced, it makes the path to truth much harder to find. However, when one steadfastly holds to the truth, even falsehood can lose its power and appear as truth in contrast.

A corporate leader's frustrating challenge is dealing with their obligation far beyond just attaining the company's financial targets. The role of the executive of the company is to also to the society at large, causing the results of their acts to be for the welfare of the community, nature, and future generations. Abiding to right conduct means harmonizing literal success and the duty to social responsibility, which helps the organizations to attain the highest levels of ethics and moral.

It is leaders who occasionally exhibit right conduct and those who manifest it in decision-making that reveal a deep commitment to the development of such values as justice, trustworthiness, and responsibility. Such principles are not only about maximizing profit but also making positive the impact of the world.

Right conduct is the path leaders follow to earn trust and loyalty—not only from employees but also from customers and investors. This trust forms the foundation of a positive organizational culture, one built on shared values and mutual respect.

Engaging Stakeholders Strategically

The concept of stakeholder engagement is based on the initiation of trust, alliance, and vision compliance with the organization's vision. Ancient wisdom is related to wisdom, clarity, and guidance which are qualities critical for wise leaderships when dealing with different categories of stakeholders such as employees, investors, customers, and communities.

This verse reminds us:

"shruyatam dharma sarvasyam shruyatam palanam tatha atmana pratikoolani paresham na samacharet"

श्रूयतां धर्मसर्वस्यं
श्रूयतां पालनं तथा।
आत्मनः प्रतिकूलानि
परेषां न समाचरेत्॥

Listen to the duty of all, and protect accordingly. Do not do unto others what would be unwelcome to yourself.

Engagement that is effective calls for differentiating people's perspectives, figuring out potential problems, and creating a warm environment to enable the courses to proceed to be mutually beneficial. Leaders should be explicit in decision-making, talk to customers regularly, and in case of need, change their strategies.

1. Building Trust through Transparent Communication

Once the key stakeholders are identified, ongoing interaction should occur through regular and transparent communication. Honest, straightforward dialogue focused on doing what is right within one's capacity is essential. Just as ancient texts emphasize clarity and truthfulness, leaders must also practice transparency in their communication. This openness enables the entire team to engage meaningfully in the decision-making process.

To make communication clearer, use different tools that can be face-to-face meetings, surveys, emails, social media interactions, and community outreach programs. Regular engagement ensures that the leaders get to know the concerns of the stakeholders thus it becomes easier to solve potential issues before they become big.

2. Collaborating to Achieve Organizational Goals

To be more precise, getting connected with the stakeholders is not only about servicing their current apprehensions but is additionally about enabling cooperation to achieve the goals that are in common. For successful businesses, the stakeholders, irrespective of whether they are employees, clients, investors, or residents of the community, are their key supporters.

A famous verse states:

na pāpam kartum icchanti satāṁ buddhir akāraṇā kṛtaṁ pāpaṁ prati naiva te tyajanti svam uttamam

न पापं कर्तुमिच्छन्ति
सतां बुद्धिरकारणा।
कृतं पापं प्रति नैव
ते त्यजन्ति स्वमुत्तमम्॥

The minds of the noble never wish to do wrong without cause; even when wronged, they do not abandon their own highest virtue.

In the corporate world, leaders first need to form an environment in which stakeholders are appreciated, involved, and encouraged to work on the long-term vision of the company.

To start with, a very productive way is through engagement of stakeholders in the decision-making processes. The leaders who openly encourage stakeholder engagement by asking for their ideas, validating constructive criticism, and inviting participation create a collective sense of ownership.

Conclusion

With the unpredictability and global connectivity of actual business reality, the participation of upholders of three stakeholders, the executive one especially, becomes a crucial factor for the realization of efficient company management. Organizations that do not manage their relationships with stakeholders practically always experience the lack of trust, and correctly so, which leads to conflicts and also affect their reputation on a more negative basis.

A verse leaves this wisdom:

"isavasyam idam sarvam yat kinca jagatyam jagat tena tyaktena bhunjitha ma gridhah kasya svid dhanam"

ईशावास्यमिदं सर्वं

यत्किञ्च जगत्यां जगत्।

तेन त्यक्तेन भुञ्जीथा

मा गृधः कस्यस्विद्धनम्॥

All this, whatever exists in this changing universe, is pervaded by the Divine. By this renunciation, you enjoy; do not covet anybody's wealth.

Ancient wisdom wields a guiding sword that helps us navigate today's challenges. Similarly, ethical leadership requires balancing the interests of all stakeholders by upholding fairness, transparency, and inclusivity as core principles in decision-making. This approach fosters trust and builds stronger relationships, where employees, clients, investors, and community members feel valued—not only seen but truly heard.

The strictly following of right conduct in taking decisions is the now of no malpractice in the constituency and thus a leader will automatically become morally and countryside responsible. The tale of a fair and just administration that is the cat perpetually manifested walking through all its nine lives when and only when those in charge regard the principle of rightness, not the desire to serve themselves but the common good.

The involvement of stakeholders in strategic ways is as important as any other thing. The secure two-way communication, addressing of conflicts, and involving of stakeholders are some of the crucial leadership tools that enable the leaders to match the stakeholder expectations with organizational goals.

The bottom line is that ancient wisdom does not only exemplify power but also it shows the way how to direct others towards a superior vision. By incorporating these universal principles, leaders can design ethical, purposeful organizations that promote the welfare of the people and the prosperity of the community.

CHAPTER 13

Change Management

In contemporary times, change is necessary. Change offers us the opportunity to grow and succeed; it is an inevitable part of life's journey. Similarly, organizations must navigate the endless waves of change just as individuals do throughout their lives. These changes can take many forms, including technological breakthroughs, market stagnation, or shifts in consumer behavior. Importantly, improvement and innovation are themselves expressions of change. The true mark of strong leadership lies in the ability to embrace and adapt to these evolving circumstances, laying the foundation for lasting success.

The ancient wisdom tells us:

"parivartan amritasya acharya"

परिवर्तनम् अमृतस्य आचार्यः

Change is the teacher of immortality.

This profound insight reminds us that embracing transformation is not merely about survival but about achieving lasting significance. Through these lessons, we discover principles for dealing with resistance, acceptance, and purposefulness in times of change. The sages teach us that we must achieve inner strength and resilience before we can succeed in guiding others through turbulence.

Leaders have a huge responsibility to push their teams and organizations through changes. Ancient wisdom talks about maintaining forward momentum while facing uncertain challenges. The principles of duty and change have a fundamental role in organizational change management. Through internal self-belief and vision, leaders are encouraged to act with conviction and clarity of purpose in the face of metamorphosis.

Managing changes is not only about responding to external forces. It is a process about preparing for the inevitable, realizing the pains and changing how we do things. Ancient teachings show us that change is a period of transformation, not a threat. Leaders who develop their teams' resilience, focus on goals and assist in developing new strategies will help organizations navigate change effectively.

This chapter explores how timeless wisdom can inform modern change management practices. By understanding these ancient principles, leaders can empower themselves and reshape their strategic processes. Such leaders will guide their teams through transitions with less difficulty, turning challenges into opportunities for increased productivity, creativity, and progress. The right approach to positive change leads to a better future when implemented with knowledge and inner strength.

Adapting to Change with Resilience

A famous verse offers this guidance:

"uttisthata jagrata prapya varan nibodhata"

उत्तिष्ठत जाग्रत प्राप्य वरान्निबोधत॥

Arise, awake, and stop not till the goal is reached.

This timeless exhortation underscores the vital role of resilience and inner strength when confronting adversity. Such wisdom offers enduring principles that leaders and organizations can embrace in overcoming challenges. It teaches us not to be captive to emotional ups and downs, but to remain steadfast with a clear focus on the goal. The core message is to diligently fulfill one's duty, refusing to be hindered by fear or uncertainty.

This universal lesson teaches us how to prepare for the unexpected. When changes occur, they often bring discomfort and resistance, but with resilience, organizations can overcome them. Instead of fixating on roadblocks, organizations should focus on opportunities to adjust and evolve. In a climate of resilience, leaders can steer their teams through continuous improvement despite unpredictable environments.

The connection to ancient wisdom in leadership is the ability to recover from setbacks and continue toward predetermined objectives despite problems. The sages admonish us to remain steady, to take responsibility with dedication and full attention. Leaders should demonstrate this to their teams, showing that resilience matters even when the path forward seems unclear.

How to Cultivate Resilience:

1. Foster a Growth Mindset

The growth mindset is integral to organizational resilience during change. It is the confidence that skills and talents can be attained through hard work, acumen, and persistence. Resilient companies view challenges as opportunities for growth. Such leaders inspire their teams to embrace learning, develop problem-solving skills, and respond positively to change.

When leaders have a growth mindset, they create environments where employees feel free to take risks and experiment without fear of judgment. Since change brings uncertainty, learning from mistakes enables organizations to build resilience. Leaders can instil this mindset by encouraging idea exchange, appreciating achievements, and offering skill development opportunities.

Furthermore, leaders who demonstrate belief in their team's ability to evolve awaken confidence and enthusiasm among employees, fostering positive engagement in the change process. This approach not only helps companies handle change efficiently but transforms organizational culture toward innovation and adaptability, critical elements for sustainability.

2. Embrace Change as Inevitable

This shloka teaches:

"yatha nadyah syandamanah samudre astam gacchanti namarupe vihaya"

यथा नद्यः स्यन्दमानाः

समुद्रे अस्तं गच्छन्ति

नामरूपे विहाय॥

Just as rivers flowing into the ocean disappear, losing their name and form.

This lesson says that alteration is a natural part of life. The sages say the cycle of creation and destruction is nature's law, and everything moves from one stage to another. This understanding transforms how we approach organizational change - not as something to oppose but as a natural process to welcome.

Companies that anticipate change as immutable prepare themselves for adaptability and growth rather than being caught unprepared. Failure to adapt typically results in fear, misconceptions, and inefficiency, hindering development. By making room for change, businesses adopt transformative thinking that is open-minded and future-directed, creating a culture of preparedness.

Organizations should view change not as a threat, but as a vital wake-up call to let go of outdated practices. Just as ancient sages advise maintaining composure in the midst of battle, companies must embrace change as an opportunity for transformation and a step closer to realizing their vision. By accepting change as a natural and necessary process, businesses showcase their greatest adaptability and strength.

3. S@upport Your Team

Organizational resilience depends on the collective ability to adapt, innovate, and persist. Leaders must support their teams with resources and training to effectively cope with change.

This shloka declares:

"sangachchhadhvam samvadadhvam sam vo manamsi janatam"

संगच्छध्वं संवदध्वं

सं वो मनांसि जानताम्॥

May you move in harmony, speak in one voice, let your minds be of one accord.

Leaders must provide their teams with knowledge and skills to handle transitions, through professional development, workshops, or training. Clear communication about the purpose of change helps teams remain committed.

Emotional support plays a vital role during times of uncertainty, when employees may feel anxious or overwhelmed. Leaders need to foster environments that encourage open communication, where team members feel safe to express their concerns. Building trust and promoting collaboration enables teams to face challenges together, rather than in isolation. By providing both practical guidance and emotional reassurance, leaders cultivate resilient and adaptable teams capable of navigating change with confidence.

People who feel supported become more receptive to change and contribute to the organization's resilience and long-term success. By addressing both practical needs and emotional concerns, leaders create an environment where change becomes an opportunity rather than a threat.

4. Stay Focused on Long-Term Goals

A famous verse states:

"tarati shokam atmavit"

तरति शोकम् आत्मवित्॥

The knower of the self, crosses over grief.

This advice helps leaders remain clear and focused during difficult times. Change brings immediate disruptions that can eclipse long-term goals, but ancient teachings remind us to complete our duty in harmony with higher purpose.

Leaders focused on long-term objectives guide organizations through transitions effectively. By visualizing future states, they make strategic rather than reactionary decisions, contributing to sustainable growth. When not caught in immediate chaos, leaders maintain steadiness, inspire confidence, and align decisions with broader organizational mission and vision.

By prioritizing long-term goals, organizations navigate uncertainty purposefully. Like sages advising us to perform duties based on responsibility, leaders must remain devoted to company vision and values, ensuring temporary setbacks don't divert from success paths.

Leading Organizations through Transformations

Transformations in technology, governance, or culture require leadership with courage and the ability to motivate. According to a famous verse:

"asato ma sad gamaya, tamaso ma jyotir gamaya, mrityor ma amritam gamaya"

असतो मा सद्गमय।

तमसो मा ज्योतिर्गमय।

मृत्योर् मा अमृतं गमय॥

Lead me from the unreal to the real, from darkness to light, from death to immortality.

Leaders must commit to their mission and persuade their teams to understand it.

Key Principles for Leading Transformations:

1. Lead with Clarity of Vision

In ancient traditions, sages emphasize understanding one's purpose.

A shloka proclaims:

"prajnanam brahma"

प्रज्ञानं ब्रह्म

Consciousness is the ultimate reality.

When changes occur, decisions become tentative, but leaders with clear vision provide direction and purpose.

For leaders guiding teams through transformation, presenting an inspiring vision is essential to align efforts toward shared goals. This vision acts as a lighthouse amidst challenges, framing problems and solutions within a larger purpose. It helps teams stay focused on the ultimate objective and alleviates fears associated with change.

Leaders must communicate this vision consistently, ensuring everyone understands their role in bringing it to life. When people feel connected to a meaningful cause, they are more likely to embrace change, offer support, and have confidence in the organization's direction. Just as ancient wisdom provides clarity of purpose, leaders must help their teams see and commit to the collective mission during times of transformation.

2. Focus on the Bigger Picture

This verse counsels:

"yat manas na manute yena ahuh mano matam"

यन्मनसा न मनुते
येनाहुर्मनो मतम्॥

That which the mind cannot think of, but because of which the mind can think. Those who rise above personal concerns can see that individual results form part of a grand design. While change brings short-term problems, leaders must maintain long-term perspective.

During change, people often fixate on immediate issues, such as market shifts, financial shortages, or employee resistance, overlooking broader contexts. Though each development stage is a stepping stone, leaders must see beyond short-term challenges to integrate obstacles into the journey.

Leaders must guide teams to focus on common goals, helping them overcome obstacles with resilience and clarity. This perspective fixes organizational gaze on final goals, ensuring that immediate challenges don't impede long-term success and development progress.

3. Involve Your Team in the Process

Change succeeds when the entire organization accepts it, not just when management imposes it.

This verse advises:

"sarve bhavantu sukhinah sarve santu niramayah"

सर्वे भवन्तु सुखिनः
सर्वे सन्तु निरामयाः॥

"May all be "happy," may all be free from disease."

True leadership embraces this spirit by empowering employees to actively participate in transformation, contribute meaningfully, and take ownership of their roles.

This approach fosters shared responsibility, builds trust, and unites teams around a common vision.

When every employee feels included, respected, and valued, their sense of competence grows, making them more engaged and supportive of change initiatives. Effective leaders actively seek team input, promoting collaboration and ensuring that every voice is heard. This collective approach cultivates a sense of togetherness and aligns individual goals with the organization's broader mission.

Team involvement creates transparency, vital for trust between leaders and employees. When people believe their input matters, they become more satisfied with organizational direction. The result is not just transformation but sustainable change built on collective effort and common purpose.

Demonstrate Adaptability

The ancient texts stress flexibility due to worldly variability. Leaders are taught to be patient through constant changes, responding without fixation on single action courses. This philosophy defines leadership in organizational transformation. Change can be unpredictable, requiring quick adaptation for triumph.

Transformation demands that leaders anchor wherever situations require; mindset shifts become essential. When customer needs, market conditions, technologies, or competition strategies emerge, businesses must adjust approaches. Narrow-minded decision-making creates myopia, while adaptability ensures competitiveness, relevance, and sustainable recovery after disruptions.

Leaders must model flexibility for their teams. When employees see management confidently adjusting strategies and embracing changes, this catalyses rapid adoption as fear transforms into trust and enjoyment. Like ancient sages teaching adaptation to changing realities, senior administrators must demonstrate flexibility for informed decisions aligned with new organizational needs and goals. This adaptability ensures efficient, sustainable transformation processes.

Conclusion

Change management through ancient wisdom is both adaptation to external shifts and a window for executive decisions, personal growth, and business planning.

This verse reminds us:

"Parivartanam jeevanam"

परिवर्तनं जीवनम्

Change is life itself.

This knowledge emphasizes building strong systems capable of facing changing times through adversity, steadfastness, and flexibility. Leaders thus move from surviving to thriving, using a resilient mindset to accomplish organizational success.

Ancient wisdom presents change alongside seasons and time - not as a terror to fight but as a companion for life, approached with an open mind and warm heart. The power of change drives enterprise evolution through vision, strategy, and organizational dynamics built on resilience, courage, and adaptability. When approached with the ability to absorb change, clarity, flexibility, and strength, it leads to productive transformation. Leaders with positive mindsets keep organizations cohesive and agile, ready for new challenges and opportunities.

Even in times of change, ancient wisdom holds true: be wise, stay the course, and remain unfazed. Managers who embody these principles provide their teams with stability and resilience, guiding them with clarity through periods of uncertainty. The most effective approach to change is to embrace it as a constructive and empowering process—one where both organizations and individuals adapt skillfully and achieve their goals, even amid the shifting winds of transformation.

CHAPTER 14

Strategic Leadership Development

In today's rapidly evolving business landscape, the success of any organization hinges on effective leadership. Decision-makers play a crucial role in steering teams toward desired outcomes, acting as visionaries who guide their organizations through challenges and inspire sustained growth. As businesses face continuous waves of technological, economic, and cultural change, the need to cultivate the next generation of leaders has become more critical than ever.

Leadership development is not solely about identifying individuals with the right skills and competencies; it also involves nurturing deeper, internal qualities that extend beyond technical expertise. Attributes such as integrity, emotional intelligence, and self-awareness are essential for building resilient, ethical, and adaptive leaders capable of driving long-term success.

The ancient wisdom found in Sanskrit texts offers a timeless guidebook for establishing strategic leaders.

This verse notes:

"vidya vinaya sampanne brahmane gavi hastini shuni chaiva shva pake cha panditah sama darshinah"

विद्या विनय सम्पन्ने
ब्राह्मणे गवि हस्तिनि।
शुनि चैव श्वपाके च
पण्डिताः समदर्शिनः॥

The truly learned see with equal vision a humble scholar, a cow, an elephant, a dog, and an outcaste.

These teachings touch upon life both in prosperity and adversity; they offer fundamental leadership principles that can be applied to all types of leadership. Decision-making is part of life and can be quite challenging. Leaders should work on emotional regulation, duty, and purpose. Ancient teachings provide insights into management, strategic thinking, ethical values and personal development.

This chapter encompasses the ancient wisdom approach to the development of leaders who embody the principles of goodness, wisdom, and resilience. The teaching focuses on developing future leaders by learning from these texts, guides of self-mastery and ethical leadership. This knowledge lays the foundation for developing leadership qualities important in conquering VUCA environments.

Leaders implementing this ancient knowledge master themselves, control their emotions, develop deep faith or Dharma with clear purpose. The wisdom of the ages requires leaders to motivate collaborative action through moral behaviour and make judgments desirable for their groups and organizations. Morally responsible leadership anchored in fairness, respect, and integrity nurtures trust and creates an environment where every team member is significant and motivated to make an impact toward common goals.

Developing Future Leaders from Ancient Teachings

Ancient texts provide essential viewpoints for tomorrow's leadership, underlining that leadership isn't just running the show, but inspiring people with purpose and honesty. The central idea is Dharma, or righteousness, as the guiding moral force in decision-making.

This principle enhances leadership training by shifting the focus from personal ambition to the broader organizational mission and values. Leaders who act in accordance with Dharma are not driven by external rewards or deterred by challenges; their motivation stems from a deep sense of duty. This approach fosters a model of ethical and resilient leadership, ensuring that future leaders remain anchored in responsibility, integrity, and moral clarity.

Key Points in Developing Future Leaders:

1. Aligning Actions with Purpose:

Ancient wisdom guides leaders on life's nature, the universe's purpose, and existence's reality.

According to this verse:

"vidya dadati vinayam vinayat yati patratam patratvaad dhanam apnoti dhanat dharmam tatah sukham"

विद्या ददाति विनयं
विनयात् याति पात्रताम्।
पात्रत्वात् धनमाप्नोति
धनात् धर्मं ततः सुखम्॥

Education gives humility, from humility one becomes worthy, from worthiness one gets wealth, from wealth one does good deeds, and from that comes joy.

This stresses upon reconditioning actions to a higher purpose. Leaders should not only produce tasks or reach objectives, but make decisions led by broader vision. The advice to leaders is to act according to duty with self-detachment from personal outcomes, focusing on excellence in Dharma duties.

For executives, this requires mental change. Leadership isn't simply about current payoffs, but about benefiting the whole organization long-term. This mission provides both daily foundation and criteria for greatness.

Visionary leaders create environments where teams feel a shared sense of responsibility toward common goals. This alignment fosters motivation, dedication, and accountability, strengthening collaboration and mutual support. By leading with integrity and a clear sense of purpose, such leaders earn trust and respect—essential foundations for building strong relationships and driving effective execution.

2. Continuous Learning and Growth:

Ancient wisdom provides moral support to disciples.

This verse teaches:

"so'kāmayata bahu syām prajāyeyeti"

स ऋकामयत बहु स्याम् प्रजायेयेति।

May I become many, may I grow forth.

Leadership isn't just making decisions and executing commands, but a journey of constant learning based on self-awareness. Sages taught disciples inner qualities enabling leadership thriving. Crucial messages include invaluable wisdom, humility, selflessness, and vision - important leadership traits.

This rule guides leaders who are aware of their development. Leadership isn't stable skills, but a flux process evolving over time. Leaders must analyse their behaviour, learn from past actions and remain open to failure and triumph insights. Leaders shouldn't stay comfortable but remain adaptable to environmental pressures. Self-awareness helps realize strengths and weaknesses, offering ground for thoughtful decisions.

Leaders must possess selflessness, emphasizing team and organizational well-being above personal accomplishment. This creates trust and respect, as leaders know what's best for others.

Companies prioritizing learning and development create leaders who not only perform well but are patient, empathetic, and skilled at guiding teams with focus and togetherness.

3. Nurturing a Learning Culture:

Ancient texts explain consistent learning and self-improvement in leadership. The Mahabharata says:

"nāsty-akṛtaḥ kṛtena"

नास्त्यकृतः कृतेन।

Nothing that has not been done before can be done now.

Leaders mentor future leaders by creating learning communities. Learning environments encourage flexibility, versatility, and confidence development. Beyond new abilities, they present frameworks attentive to diverse ideas, revelations, and experiences.

Leaders who make employees lifelong students create environments supporting learning, innovation, and personal development. They help employees view problems as growth opportunities rather than obstacles. In secure environments, mistakes become lessons and experiments proceed without disapproval fear, helping team members identify and surpass limitations.

Leaders encouraging learning cultures invest in resources, tools, and education opportunities through training programs, mentoring, and knowledge sharing platforms. Those adapting to changes learn and grow well, and when leaders cultivate such environments, they arm teams with supreme tools to overcome obstacles with resilience.

Learning cultures develop adaptable, proactive, resilient leaders which are all crucial skills for today's dynamic business environment. Those stimulating learning cultures not only care for business but enlarge and enrich it amid changing times.

Self-Mastery as a Leadership Trait

Effectual leadership consists in leading with confidence and agility when facing challenges.

According to a famous verse:

"mano hi dvividham proktam shuddham cha ashuddham eva cha ashuddham kama sankalpam shuddham kama vivarjitam"

मनो हि द्विविधं प्रोक्तं

शुद्धं चाशुद्धमेव च।

अशुद्धं कामसङ्कल्पं
शुद्धं कामविवर्जितम्॥

The mind is said to be of two types - pure and impure. The impure mind is filled with desires while the pure mind is free from desires.

Sages stressed mastering mind, emotions, and desires, arguing that those commanding internals stay steady amid chaos. Leaders exercising self-control aren't overwhelmed by impulses, pressure, or insecurity, thus thinking, reasoning and acting during crises. This control allows managing one's state, promoting trust with followers.

They help teams stay grounded and focused, even in the face of uncertainty or adversity. Modern leaders harness everyday challenges not just to fuel their own growth, but to inspire their teams toward excellence. By navigating obstacles with clarity and purpose, they model effective leadership and empower others to rise above the odds.

Key Aspects of Self-Mastery in Leadership:

1. Emotional Regulation:

Emotional management is crucial in leadership, and ancient wisdom unlocks novel methods for this. Leaders surrendering to negative emotions may make harmful, hasty decisions affecting organization and team dynamics. Anger, greed, and fear obstruct good judgment, causing wrong decisions with adverse long-term results. Ancient teachings emphasize staying calm and wise regardless of external circumstances. Calm leaders judge situations accurately, follow others' viewpoints, and provide wise guidance.

The manager's emotional regulation develops the team's emotional intelligence. When leaders control emotions, people feel safe expressing themselves and sharing ideas freely. Calm, perceptive leaders create less tensed teams, able to work through inevitable problems.

Ancient meditation teachings pressure leaders. Leadership requires self-regulation, particularly emotional, building leadership on calmness, clarity, and wisdom.

Inspiring Collective Action through Ethical Leadership

In ancient texts, sages emphasize ethical practices for leaders. A famous verse teaches:

"yadā pañcāvatiṣṭhante jñānāni manasā saha buddhiś ca na viceṣṭati tām āhuḥ paramāṃ gatim"

यदा पञ्चावतिष्ठन्ते
ज्ञानानि मनसा सह।
बुद्धिश्च न विचेष्टते
तामाहुः परमां गतिम्॥

When the five senses and the mind are stilled, and reason itself rests in silence, then begins the highest path.

This profound wisdom highlights that true leadership begins with inner stillness and moral clarity. For sages, moral uprightness is rooted in sincerity, trustworthiness, and justice—qualities that are upheld irrespective of changing circumstances. Successful leaders, guided by the principles of Dharma, act responsibly and ethically, prioritizing duty over personal gain or recognition.

Ethical leadership fosters a culture grounded in fairness, honesty, and transparency, inspiring others to emulate these values. When leaders consistently model integrity in both word and action, they establish strong ethical standards across the organization. Such moral consistency not only builds trust and respect but also lays the foundation for responsible, resilient, and ultimately successful institutions.

Principles of Ethical Leadership:

1. Leading by Example:

Leaders significantly influence ethical behaviour, prompting collective action and virtue-oriented culture. A leader's well-being has a profound impact on their team. Employees thrive when they are guided by inspiring leadership, not by actions that leave them feeling embarrassed. It's essential for leaders to foster an environment that motivates and uplifts everyone, creating a culture of confidence and collaboration. This manifests especially where trust is paramount, as people follow leaders brave enough to clearly state intentions. When leaders take fair, transparent approaches, they inspire others to treat each other without prejudice, creating participative and just environments.

Ethical leaders inspire confidence as role models. Their ability to display resilience and insight, handling diverse conflict or decision situations fairly and respectfully, offers visible guidance for team members to follow similarly. This develops strong team bonds and mutual accountability atmospheres, making everyone feel necessary for company ethics.

Conclusion

With teachings of wisdom, purpose and ethical responsibility, ancient Sanskrit wisdom provides a remarkable leadership framework beyond traditional management techniques. These teachings about wisdom, purpose, and ethical responsibility are necessary ingredients for effective strategic leadership. Leaders merging these lessons into their philosophy better face challenges, motivate, and nurture continuous growth and self-improvement cultures.

Becoming tomorrow's leaders necessitates purpose-driven leadership bedrock. A famous verse declares:

"satyameva jayate"

सत्यमेव जयते

Truth alone triumphs.

This verse highlights aligning actions with duty rather than personal gains. Leaders knowing organizations' greater missions motivate teams to work with dedication and purpose toward that mission. This clear vision guides organizations to stay resilient and adaptable amid uncertainties.

Ancient wisdom relates self-mastery to leadership's foremost objective. Leaders exemplifying self-discipline, emotional regulation, and continuous self-improvement inspire their teams. Calm, honest leaders instil organizational trust and solidity. This internal fortitude equips leaders with complete perspective to provide direction during change with courage.

Finally, ethical leadership begins making success sustainable. Leaders advocating uprightness, transparency, and integrity access collective action and create trust and collaboration cultures. By creating work environments promoting ethical behaviour, organizations develop strong relationships with employees, stakeholders, and customers.

Leaders can transform their leadership styles by understanding ancient texts' wisdom and succeed in their jobs without mistakes, bringing meaning to their organizations.

CHAPTER 15

Risk Management

Risk management is an important part of strategic leadership, as it ensures that organizations can go through uncertainty and stay in line with their long-term goals. Ancient Sanskrit wisdom rhythms a profound intelligence about controlling risks namely nonattachment, foresight, and courage.

These teachings direct leaders to deal with risks without the clouded perception of their minds, with clarity, wisdom, and the only acceptance informed decisions can be made while they are committed to their *'mission'*.

In today's fast-moving and totally unpredictable business world, the risk is something that is beyond our control, and it can be either the brick wall of the progress of a company or a stepping stone toward the company's expansion. Many organizations face the uncertainty that results from the paradox of trying to avoid making mistakes while at the same time creating an environment for innovation. Ancient wisdom sets a refreshing view on the management of risk that is upholding a perspective of simplicity, courage, and the sense of ethics as the centre of it. The executives who embrace these principles can deal with the risks having certainty and knowing their decisions are based on their clear reasoning and not the emotions of fear.

The matter of risk in ancient texts is not the simple avoidance of losses rather it is about facing the predicament with an open and honest mind. This verse declares:

"yato hasta tato drishtih yato drishtih tato manah"

यतो हस्त: तत: दृष्टि:
यतो दृष्टि: तत: मन:॥

Where the hands go, the eyes follow; where the eyes go, the mind follows.

This reflects the idea that actions, attention, and intentions are deeply interconnected. In a world where outcomes are often uncertain, resilience and sharp thinking are key to navigating ambiguity. Executives who blend optimism with strategic foresight are better equipped to turn challenges into opportunities, paving the way for long-term sustainability and growth. In this context, risk management evolves beyond mere vigilance; it becomes an act of courage and clarity. It involves confronting challenges directly while upholding ethical values and aligning with the organization's strategic goals.

This section focuses on three areas of risk management: detachment and acceptance, strategic foresight, and managing uncertainty together with resilience. By implementing these guiding ideas into the leadership and decision-making, institutions are able to develop a strong foundation that not only reduces the risk but also turns the potential pitfalls into opportunities for sustainable growth.

Detachment and Acceptance in Risk Management

Understanding Detachment in Decision-Making

Ancient wisdom teaches that being truly wise consists in acting with full dedication and forgoing expectations about the outcome. This verse advises:

"na me bandho'sti mokso va bhrantih shanta nirashraya"

न मे बन्धोऽस्ति मोक्षो वा

भ्रान्तिः शान्ता निराश्रया॥

I have neither bondage nor liberation; all confusion has been dispelled.

The leaders are often confronted with difficult decisions that can have an important impact on them. Their attachment to the result that they believe in might unnecessarily cloud their judgment. By concentrating on the process and not the fear of failure, leaders can objectively measure risks and make the expected moves that will position their organization for the future.

Decision-making in serious scenarios needs objectivity and emotional control. This is a valuable lesson to the present time where the decision-makers often struggle with immediate short-term outcomes. A leader, who is very attached to specific results, may at times find it difficult to take these risks which are needed and/or may become emotional when facing challenges. On the other hand, a leader that has no attachment can think through risks logically, adjust to new circumstances and make decisions that are best for the company in the long run.

Detachment is not the same as indifference or lack of responsibility. It implies that a person is wise enough to act right and at the same time accept the outcomes that are dependent on several if not many factors which are beyond control. Leaders who master the skill of this create an atmosphere in which their teams can take the risks that are calculated knowing that failure is not the end of everything. This nurtures a culture of innovation and resilience needed for successfully mastering intricate settings in business.

Overcoming Fear and Resistance to Risk

Risk management is inherently complex, with fear often standing as one of its greatest barriers—whether it's fear of failure, financial loss, or reputational harm. While effective leaders must acknowledge uncertainty, they cannot allow it to hinder decisive action. By accepting that risk is an unavoidable aspect of any endeavor, organizations can adopt a proactive and strategic approach, preparing for potential challenges rather than being overwhelmed by them.

Fear can frequently lead to indecision, then it keeps them from prospering and being inventive. Leaders who practice the mindset of acceptance as a basic drive, shift the view from fear-based avoidance to opportunity generating action. Rather than considering risk as a danger to any project, they may recognize it as a necessary part of development. Once their leaders become the embodiment of courage and clearness, their individuals with become unequipped to confront any ambiguities with assurance.

Through recognizing and talking to fear directly, organizations can instil an environment that is prone to taking calculated risks and that looks at failure as a learning opportunity. This thinking allows the enterprises to welcome new technologies, study new markets, adapt to change, and therefore not being haunted by the fear of failure.

Balancing Rationality and Intuition

Wisdom in risk management comes from both knowledge and intuition. Since risks often involve uncertainty, sound human judgment becomes essential for making the right decisions.

Using the data of the case together with the theory of emotional intelligence, the leader can make rational decisions and not the logical choices, which easily are reliable. With the data, the rational interpretation is possible on the topic of the chances of risks. They trust the economy, ratings, technology, and bonds for the possibility of success, and they make decisions based on the possibility of success, measured by these tools.

At the same time, the notion of ancient wisdom is that wisdom does not come only through logic. The person who possesses the gift of intuition gets to sense or his heart leads him the way, making decisions without a long thought. In high-stakes environments where vital feedback may be not all be there, managers must listen to their intuition.

By the combination of both common sense and intuition the leaders are able to find a middle way. When they stick on data they may get into the trap of over-analysing, thus, they would not be able to take action. While on the other hand, solely following intuition might mean that a person would make hasty decisions without considering the essential information. A combination of logic and intuition where both are supportive of each other is a means of achieving proper orientation between the points of wisdom, thus they can efficiently deal with risk.

Foresight and Risk Assessment Strategies

Developing Strategic Foresight

This verse advises:

> ***"sukhasya moolam dharmah***
> ***dharmasya moolam arthah"***
>
> **सुखस्य मूलं धर्मः**
> **धर्मस्य मूलं अर्थः॥**

The root of happiness is dharma (righteousness), the root of dharma is artha (economic prosperity).

This teaching is a close reflection of the concept of strategic foresight in leadership. To be transformative, a leader needs to possess the foresight to be able to sense the dangers and opportunities of the future as if from a higher plane of vision and know that present conditions are only part of the larger pattern of change. Strategic foresight is about forecasting and, in a sense, creating the future that allows organizations to detect potential interruptions before they develop into a crisis.

Leaders who cultivate foresight actively monitor external factors such as technological advancements, economic trends, and shifting market conditions. By staying attuned to changes in consumer behavior, geopolitical dynamics, and emerging innovations, they are able to detect patterns and signals that often go unnoticed by others. This forward-thinking approach empowers them to make well-informed decisions and craft long-term strategies that drive sustainable growth and innovation.

One of the main components of strategic foresight is not just being able to forecast problems but also seeing possibilities within those problems. A new technology that emerges, for instance, might destroy existing business models but it could also be the engine for innovation and development. Leaders can be the ones to steer change and lead organizations to a better path even if the potential threats can be turned into opportunities if they approach them from a positive perspective.

Scenario Planning and Contingency Strategies

An intelligent person should perceive the possibility of danger even from a friend, and the possibility of good even from an enemy. This means to be mentally prepared for different outcomes, and that one should always consider an option not to pan out as planned. In other words, this teaching illustrates the significance of scenario planning in leadership and risk management. Without refusing to accept the inevitability of certain things, an entrepreneur should be on guard and prompt enough not to get carried away with issues that might be beyond his control all of a sudden.

Scenario planning is a popular method that involves the development of different ideas about the way a particular situation that might occur in the future could develop e.g. the best-case, worst-case, and intermediary scenarios, and in that way, one can be ready for all of them. Working alongside scenario planning, devising contingency strategies is essential. These are alternative plans that could still be implemented in case one of the situations happens differently than what was expected. Utilizing existing contingency plans, companies can be flexible in their responses without losing the momentum when new situations arise.

The main message of ancient wisdom is questioning the power of poise and scheduling against undefined reality. Just as a warrior's agility is required, corporate managers, too, must spring to action and take swift decisions when unexpected developments arise. Both a company that does scenario planning and use of contingency strategies are not only protected from risks but also ready to benefit from new opportunities in the uncertainty of the future.

Managing Uncertainty with Strategic Foresight

Embracing Uncertainty as a Constant

Instead of fighting or fearing these tremendous powers, the sages make the following statement with great clarity of purpose; to take them as inevitable and to strive to live a life not just of a fulfilment of daily activities but the highest ways of existence.

Modern leadership is a field where change is the one driving thing, and it is what leaders have to get used to. This wisdom is really relevant to modern leadership since change is always the case in highly competitive businesses with short life cycles and ever-more dynamic external environments.

Leaders who think that uncertainty prevents them from doing their best are often lost and unable to do anything because they do not know what reality looks like. On the contrary, ancient lessons recommend a change in perception - top managers should be led by the fact that the unpredictable is neither to fear nor, as a result, to separate from the business world. The phenomenon of managing uncertainty allows organizations to deal with trials with more durability and quickness - a quality which is absent when the perils encounter.

Building a Resilient Organizational Culture

During times of uncertainty, the real backbone of an organization is not just the one that you keep and you are fine but also it helps you to develop and grow. To achieve success in both facing what lies ahead as well as overcoming setbacks, it is essential to construct a culture of resilience within the organization. Yes, the cultivation of resilience is an emotional experience but it is also learning the right skills, sharing the experiences, and receiving appropriate support that will not only enable the employees to see the adversity but also to face it with confidence and creativity.

One of the key drivers of success is equipping team members with the skills and training necessary to perform effectively under pressure. Equally important is fostering a culture that encourages creativity and rational problem-solving, an essential yet often overlooked component of organizational resilience. Forward-thinking organizations actively motivate and incentivize their employees to adopt diverse perspectives and think innovatively, recognizing that breakthrough solutions rarely emerge from conventional thinking alone.

Creating a psychologically safe work environment where individuals feel empowered to take risks and speak up is critical. When employees feel trusted and supported, they are more inclined to share new ideas and offer constructive solutions, confident that their input will be valued. A culture grounded in open communication, collaboration, and mutual respect not only fosters innovation but also enables organizations to navigate uncertainty and emerge stronger from adversity.

The Role of Ethical Leadership in Risk Management

This verse teaches:

"satyam bruyat priyam bruyat na bruyat satyam apriyam"

सत्यं ब्रूयात् प्रियं ब्रूयात्
न ब्रूयात् सत्यं अप्रियम्॥

Speak the truth, speak what is pleasant. Do not speak the truth which is unpleasant.

Such a form of moral decision-making becomes important for embracing trust, credibility, and organizational sustainability not only in the present but in the future as well. In stressful and unstable situations, the decisions of the leaders will usually be put under the microscope, and their ethical choices will mainly determine the organization's reputation and its stability.

Ethical leadership requires making decisions that are not only strategically sound but are also moral as well in the same way, even when the decision-making process is confrontational or the road ahead is not clear. Ancient wisdom tells that the leaders should work based on their purpose and values so that their decisions will not just be for the best of the organization but also the community and other people. Through obeisance to the guidelines of high ethics, leaders anchor in a habitat of confidence, where the substitute team-members, payers, recruiters, as well as business partners, are sure that decisions have been made with integrity.

Conclusion

As interpreted in ancient wisdom, it offers deep understanding into wisdom, detachment, and foresight as aspects of risk management. The lessons from the sages are centred on the fact that uncertainty is an irrevocable part of life, and how we embrace it is what leads to our achievement. Incorporating the fundamentals of strategic foresight, leaders are, thus, able to prophesy encumbrances in advance and, thereby, prevent their organizations from being taken aback. It is through this kind of prediction that these inventions can apart from risks also work in a way to enable the companies to modify themselves and act confidently in a rapidly changing environment.

Similarly, rational analysis and intuition are of utmost importance. On the one hand, the application of data and logical reasoning maps the risks; on the other hand, intuition provides the natural guidance that very often results in well-timed and well-thought-out decisions. Ancient wisdom makes guiding that leaders should neither rely solely on one or the other but the two could be combined in such a way that more holistic and agile decisions are taken.

Creating a solid organizational culture is a must. They set the goal of leader who are of a growth mindset, those who promote innovation and new technology through learning from their mistakes, and the ones who render set-backs as the foundation for development. This strength is the stability that makes organizations capable of surviving uncertainty and going then onwards of troubles even in a tough environment.

To crown it all, ancient philosophy shows that risk management is not only minding off or mitigating the risks; rather the potential for transformation and growth is to be embraced within every situation. By adjusting the perspective, the CEOs can be transformed from the uncertainty to becoming the one who causes abundant future growth and greatness, and so the organizations too will be that way, sustaining themselves, staying flexible, and keeping the environment, they are in to be the changing one's head.

Conclusion

As we conclude our exploration of strategic thinking through the lens of the Bhagavad Gita, we stand at a unique intersection of ancient wisdom and modern business practice. Through fifteen dimensions of strategy, we've witnessed how teachings delivered on an ancient battlefield offer profound guidance for today's organizational challenges. This convergence is not coincidental but reflects the universal nature of human endeavour, leadership, and strategic thinking across millennia.

The journey we've taken reveals that effective strategy is not merely an intellectual exercise but a holistic practice encompassing mental clarity, emotional resilience, ethical foundation, and skilful action. From the foundational concepts of purpose clarity and detachment from results, through the practical applications of delegation and conflict resolution, to the organizational dimensions of stakeholder management and risk assessment, we've seen how the Gita's principles create a comprehensive framework for strategic excellence.

Perhaps the most powerful insight from this exploration is that strategic mastery begins with self-mastery. The leader who wishes to navigate organizational complexity must first navigate their own internal landscape. Clarity of purpose, detachment from outcomes, adaptability in thinking, resilience under pressure, ethical steadfastness, and focused attention. These are not just organizational capabilities but personal ones. The Gita teaches us that external achievements flow from internal development, that organizational transformation begins with leader transformation.

This insight challenges conventional approaches to strategy development that focus primarily on external analysis, competitive positioning, and resource allocation. While these remain important, the Gita suggests they must be complemented by the development of the strategist themselves. The leader with a clear mind, steady purpose, and ethical compass will naturally make better strategic choices than one clouded by confusion, attachment, or moral ambiguity.

As we face increasingly volatile, uncertain, complex, and ambiguous business environments, this integrated approach to strategy becomes not just beneficial but essential. The accelerating pace of technological change, shifting geopolitical landscapes, environmental challenges, and evolving stakeholder expectations create a perfect storm that conventional strategic approaches struggle to navigate. In this context, the timeless wisdom of the Gita offers not just philosophical comfort but practical guidance.

The fifteen chapters of this book provide a framework for development that integrates the external and internal dimensions of strategy. They offer both philosophical depth and practical application, ancient wisdom and contemporary relevance. Yet this framework is not prescriptive but adaptative; it invites leaders to discover their own path of strategic development rather than imposing a rigid methodology.

As you apply these principles in your leadership journey, remember that, like Arjuna, you stand at your own Kurukshetra. Your own field of dharma where duty, action, and purpose converge. The challenges you face are unique to your context, yet the principles for navigating them are universal. The wisdom that guided warriors millennia ago can guide executives today, not because business is warfare, but because both domains require clarity of purpose, ethical action, and steadiness of mind.

The strategic journey is never complete. Each achievement creates new challenges, each answer generates new questions. Yet with the Gita's wisdom as our foundation, we can approach this ongoing journey with confidence, clarity, and purpose. May these simplified strategy skills serve as your compass as you navigate the complexity of modern leadership, bringing ancient wisdom to bear on tomorrow's challenges.